Night Games! is hilarious, yet very informative. I could not put it down!

—London Bridges, author
101 Ways Men Cheat and How to Catch Them!

Rodney Battles keeps it real and provides a true glimpse into the nightclub and bar scene. If you want to know how men and women really think and act, what appeals to the opposite sex, what turns men and women on and off, and what attracts the sexes to each another, *Night Games!* is mandatory reading! This book is the nightclub version of "male/female sexploration."

—Ella Patterson, author
Will The Real Women Please Stand Up?

Every man who has trouble meeting women in nightclubs will benefit from this book!

—Don Diebel, singles expert, author
president, Gemini Publishing Company, Houston, TX

The author has provided valuable insights into how men and women think and behave in nightclubs and bars.

—Susan Rabin, director, www.schoolofflirting.com;
author, *101 Ways to Flirt* and *How to Attract Anyone, Anytime, Anyplace.*

Night Games!

Night Games!

A Guide to Understanding and Enjoying the Nightclub and Bar Scene

Rodney A. Battles

Brown Books Dallas

Night Games! —

A Guide to Understanding and Enjoying the Nightclub and Bar Scene

Printed and bound in the United States of America

ISBN 0-9715113-0-6 LCCN 2001119117

For information, contact

Brown Books
16200 N. Dallas Parkway, Suite 225
Dallas, Texas 75248
www.brownbooks.com

First printing 2002

Acknowledgments

This book would not have been written without the contributions and encouragement of my nail technician, Carla. I've had a standing appointment with her every other Saturday for seven years. Several years ago, Carla was a dancer and a regular at her favorite country/western clubs. She was also the first female born into her family in fifty-two years. During my Saturday visits to the salon, we have talked about every aspect of male/female relationships, often attracting the interest and participation of other patrons. Carla's experience, insight, wisdom, and wit are reflected throughout this book.

I acknowledge my favorite club managers, bartenders and waitresses, and bouncers. Thanks, Chris, Todd, Kevin, Brad, Scott, Melissa, Dee, Charles, and Bryan for always treating me like a VIP.

Also, I would like to acknowledge my favorite deejays, Roger, Katy "The DJ Lady," Carl, and Randall. Thanks for all the times you have played our "special" requests, especially the *Electric Slide.*

A special acknowledgment goes to relationship expert

Don Diebel, president and owner of Gemini Publishing Company. He publishes *The Don Diebel "Succeed With Women" Newsletter* on the Internet (http://www.getgirls.com). Don has been a guest speaker on several TV and radio shows, and he has been featured in print interviews. I highly recommend his newsletter and books offered on his Web site.

I would like to acknowledge the friends and acquaintances with whom I have enjoyed the club experience over the years. You know who you are. I have shared some of your comments and anecdotes in this book. As promised, I have not included any of the stories that would prevent you from running for public office!

Finally, I am grateful to the wonderful team of professionals that I have been fortunate enough to work with on this book. I thank Milli Brown, Kathryn Grant, Suzanna Brown, and the exceptional Brown Books team for the design and layout of the book, for mentoring me throughout the entire publishing process, and for believing in me. I thank my publicists, Aric Caplan, Audra Berman, Brian Feinblum, and the Planned Television Arts team for recognizing the potential for this book, sharing my vision and passion, and for conducting a flawless national media campaign. I also thank Marianne Bohr, Jen Linck, and the Biblio Distribution team for their excellent work to sell and distribute *Night Games!* to the book trade. I could not have asked for a better team!

Contents

Preface

Although it is purely coincidental that the initials of my name in reverse order spell BAR, I have enjoyed the club scene for over fifteen years. Contrary to popular belief, clubs and bars are not the meat markets they are purported to be. They are more accurately a source of ego-battering rejection, frustration, and humiliation for men—and a source of unwanted attention, overt sexual advances, and negative energy for women. Conventional methods of meeting the opposite sex do not apply to the "unnatural" and "contrived" settings in clubs and bars.

Despite the negative publicity that clubs and bars have received, they continue to provide more opportunity for men and women ages twenty-one to fifty to meet and have fun on Friday and Saturday nights than do any other venues. Why do men and women go to clubs and bars? Why do some enjoy the club experience more than others?

I have two key observations on this point. First, men and women who have fun and do well at meeting the opposite sex in clubs and bars have different attitudes from those who don't. Second, they also know where to go and when, have realistic expectations, and know how men and women think, act, and react in an environment that is not naturally conducive to meeting someone.

Night Games! unravels the club scene conundrum, and reveals how and why we do the things we do. Men and women who follow the principles, tips, techniques, and rules of thumb that I have outlined will find themselves more comfortable in these settings, be more successful in meeting other men and women, and, as a consequence, have more fun.

Although much of the information in this book can be used in other places and situations, it is presented here as it applies specifically to the gender interaction in clubs and bars.

Chapter 1

Where to Go and When

Men and women generally select a club or bar based on its proximity to where they live or work, the type of music played there, the ethnicity of its patrons, or the age of the crowd the club or bar attracts. Possibilities include the following:

Brewpubs
Dance Clubs
Hotel Clubs and Lounges
Cigar/Martini Bars
Jazz Clubs
Karaoke Bars
Piano Bars
Sports Bars
Wine Bars

Popular dance clubs may have a deejay, a live band, or both that play the following types of music:

Alternative
Blues
Country/Western
House/Techno
Old School R&B
Rap/Hip Hop
Reggae
Tejano/Latin
Urban/Top 40

If you like to dance, select a club with a deejay who plays music for the crowd. The deejay's role is crucial in a club where people dance. Some deejays play standard formats and will not change to suit the crowd. Clubs make money by selling alcohol. A good deejay will keep patrons on the dance floor because the more they dance, the more they will spend buying drinks.

If you are a man, it should not be obvious that your primary objective is to pick up women! This will be explained later. If you do want to meet women, however, you should select clubs that provide a mix of fast and slow dance music played by a deejay or a live band. The club should also provide an atmosphere where women can feel relatively safe and comfortable. Clubs that have valet parking, security, and comfortable seating are more appealing to women than clubs that don't offer these amenities.

If you are a woman whose primary objective is to meet men, it really doesn't matter what clubs you choose. Men will be there. If you desire to meet A-list men, however, you should select clubs that attract a variety of professional and nonprofessional men and have strict dress codes.

Rule of Thumb . . .

Select clubs and bars where you fit in with their clientele.

There are two types of crowds in the more popular

clubs on Friday nights. Happy hour groups usually occupy clubs from 6:00 P.M. to 9:00 P.M. Between 9:00 and 10:00, the crowd changes and by 10:30 or 11:00 is out in full force. Friday is the best night to party and meet someone in a club where many regulars go. The competition to meet women, however, is tough on Fridays. Men generally outnumber women by a ratio of six to one. Married men are more likely to visit clubs on Friday night because it is easier for them. They can usually justify getting out then and get permission from their wives to go out with the boss, customers, or a group of fellas from the office for a couple of drinks.

Local radio station personalities occasionally make special appearances on Friday nights at some of the more popular dance clubs in large cities. There is always a higher ratio of women to men in a club on these nights. Expect the club to be extremely crowded with men and women who are dressed to impress. If the club is located in a city that has a major sports franchise, athletes may also be there. They, of course, will get attention from most of the women, and it may be more difficult for the average man to meet women in the club on these nights.

Saturday night is date night, so more couples will likely choose this night to go out dancing. Women who are uncomfortable with the Friday night crowds at some clubs may go out on Saturday because there is usually less pressure from men looking to pick up women. Saturday night is also the night a group of female friends are most likely to choose for a “girls’ night out.” Extremely popular dance clubs are an exception. They will draw large crowds of single men and women on Saturday as well as Friday nights.

Bartenders, waitresses, bouncers, and regulars agree that men and women behave differently when there is a full moon on the weekend. People are more uninhibited on these nights. Many men believe that women are sexually in heat when the moon is full.

Wednesdays or Thursdays are designated as Ladies’ Night at many clubs. On these nights, women can drink very inexpensively. The popularity of Ladies’ Night varies greatly between clubs, as some will attract many women on these nights, while others will not. Women who work days will usually go out on Ladies’ Night between 6:00 P.M. and 9:00 P.M., and women who work weekends may also go out for a little fun at this time.

Have you ever wondered when and where the waitresses, bartenders, and deejays go to dance and have fun? Most clubs do not permit their waitstaffs to party at the club where they work. Since many clubs are closed on Sundays or Mondays, employees from one or more clubs will party on these nights at a special spot that usually does not have too many outsiders. If you get to know the waitstaff at a club, you may have a good chance to party with them on their nights off.

Clubs or lounges that are located in the larger hotels and have a deejay or a live band and a dance floor are good places to meet divorcees, widows, and professional women from thirty to fifty years old. The atmosphere here is more intimate than in the large dance clubs. Women who frequent these clubs on weekends are generally interested in meeting quality men. They aren't looking for a man to take care of them financially, and they don't play the games that are played by young people at the crowded and popular nightspots.

Robert enjoys meeting women during the week in upscale hotel clubs and lounges. According to him, "professional women generally travel into a city on Mondays and Tuesdays, and they generally leave on Wednesdays or Thursdays." If they stay at one of the city's better hotels, they are usually comfortable stopping in for a cocktail after their workday is over or for a nightcap after dinner. The atmosphere in upscale hotel clubs and lounges is very relaxed, there is comfortable seating, and they are not crowded. Robert may arrive between 6:00 P.M. and 7:00 P.M., before business travelers normally leave to have dinner. Sometimes he waits until 8:30 P.M. or 9:00 P.M. to meet women after they return from dinner. He always wears either a suit or a sports coat. He knows that professional women who are visiting the city are likely to be dressed in business attire. "The only disadvantage to meeting professional women this way," says Robert, "is I often have to provide a legitimate explanation why I am in a hotel club in the city in which I live. If the hotel is near an airport, I usually use the excuse that I just took my boss to the airport to catch a plane and stopped in for a drink on my way home. If the hotel is not near the airport, my explanation might be I had a business meeting at the hotel earlier and thought I would have a drink before I headed home."

Robert is very comfortable around classy women, and they tend to be comfortable around him. He is a great conversationalist and doesn't come on to the women he meets. He does, however, always give out his business card before he leaves. "This way, a woman is able to contact me by phone or e-mail if she is interested."

Another important advantage in going to clubs and lounges located in the nicer hotels is that a room is available if you have too much to drink or if you are successful in meeting a woman who would like to spend the night with you. A disadvantage in going to hotel clubs is that prostitutes are sometimes there.

Rule of Thumb . . .
Men should have some casual clothes, a pair of tennis shoes or sandals, and a travel bag in the trunk of their car, if they go to hotel clubs.

It's always a good idea for a man to have a change of clothes and a travel bag when he goes out for the night. Clean underwear, a pair of jeans, a shirt, a pair of tennis shoes, and a travel bag with comb, toothbrush, toothpaste, and condoms can come in handy. If a woman asks why you just happen to have these things in your trunk, you can tell her that you keep these things with you in case you decide to spend the night at a hotel to keep from driving home under the influence of alcohol. You may also tell her that you keep a change of clothes with you in case you have car trouble and have to walk somewhere or fix the car.

Chapter 2

How Men Think in Clubs and Bars

Meeting women in clubs and bars is a ***chore*** for most men. They feel pressured to ask women to dance, initiate conversation, and flirt. This pressure, coupled with competition, can easily rob a man of three things that are necessary for his well-being: the need to be in control, the need to have his ego boosted, and the need to achieve.

The anxiety can be so great that some men wear lucky underwear or carry other good luck charms in hopes that fate will favor them on a Friday or Saturday night.

The fear of rejection is greater for men in clubs and bars than it is in other places. After all, men think that these are supposed to be places to pick up women. Actually, most men will not even ask a woman to dance because they fear rejection. They take this personally, and there is no rejection greater than being unable to dance at a club. I have watched many men leave a club after asking two or three women to dance and receiving no for an answer. If the majority of men in a club or bar are afraid to ask women to dance, how can they actually meet women? Why do men subject themselves to the ego-battering experience of clubs and bars? There are two reasons:

1. Men like variety. Clubs and bars offer a variety of visual treats.
2. The possibility of getting lucky and meeting a woman always exists.

Imagine a man having a drink early one evening while sitting at the bar in a club. Attractive twin sisters come in and also sit at the bar. They order drinks for themselves and before long, the three are talking. As the conversation progresses, the man becomes very interested in one of the twins. Which one is he most likely interested in? After all, they look exactly alike!

Rule of Thumb . . .

All other things being equal, a man will pursue a woman whom he thinks is available.

In the above scenario, if one of the twins seems more interested, she will appear to be more available. This is often enough to encourage a man to pursue a woman.

Men have a hunter mentality, and in clubs and bars, there are two types of hunters. One is aggressive. He intends to pursue and catch something. The second type is not as aggressive but will pursue when baited. The man in the scenario above is the second type of hunter.

Although women usually don't mind receiving some attention from men in clubs and bars, they hate being hit on relentlessly by men who don't interest them. Why do some men overpursue? There are two primary reasons. Since clubs and bars are considered pickup places, a woman's mere presence suggests that she is available. Some women will be pursued for this reason alone. If a man thinks she is available and interested, he will most likely pursue her. For instance, when women accept an invitation to dance or accept a drink, most men will interpret their acceptance as a sign of interest, and the hunt is on! Some women are willing to dance simply because they don't like to be rude. After all, they are in a dance club! Others will allow men to buy them drinks because they don't have to spend their money. Generally, however, men will read more into women's actions and will attempt to pursue them for the wrong reasons.

Rule of Thumb . . .

A hunter will pursue only what he thinks he can catch.

If a man asks a woman to dance, she might try to be courteous and say,

- "Not right now, maybe later."
- "I need a couple of drinks before I can dance."
- "No, thank you, I don't dance very well."

Any of these responses will give a man hope. Often, this is enough for some men to continue their pursuit.

Shy men go to clubs in hopes of being picked up by a woman. They usually have little experience with women. Consequently, they are afraid of them. Like most men, a shy man is afraid of rejection, but if he gets the nerve to approach a woman and is rejected, he will blame himself. Shy men are also afraid a woman will say yes. If she responds to his approach, another form of anxiety occurs.

Although men are the so-called stronger sex, women possess more control and power in clubs and bars. Many men simply will not expose the fragile part of their ego to a woman, unless they have reason to believe mutual interest exists, or they are drunk. Since women are in a position of control, most men think it is only fair for women to take some of the risk and make the first move. The problem with thinking this way is that women are conditioned to avoid making direct moves on a man; it is simply unladylike. Women do, however, provide hints when they are interested in a man, and herein lies an important fact.

Rule of Thumb . . .

Usually men do not catch hints very well but will respond to direct signals. If a hint is too subtle, a man's normal fears will prevail.

All men have preferences when it comes to meeting women in clubs and bars. Generally, they will move in the direction of their preferences. Men also have their minimum standards. Although their preferences do not change, *their minimum standards do!*

If a woman who does not meet a man's minimum standards is too aggressive, he will feel that he is being hunted rather than being the hunter himself. When a man feels cornered, he may act irrationally.

Rule of Thumb . . .

Men want to be seduced but not chased.

A man, whom I will refer to as Mr. Lucky, is usually at a particular club on Fridays and Saturdays. We missed him one weekend when he was out of town attending the wedding of one of his brothers. He returned home Sunday afternoon and decided to stop by the club that evening for a couple of drinks. Since Sundays are pretty dead at the club, he wasn't thinking of meeting a woman. When he entered, there were fewer than twenty people present. He took a seat at a table near the deejay's booth and ordered a drink. While he was enjoying his drink and talking with the deejay, he noticed a woman sitting alone at a table on the other side of the club. When the deejay played the Rick James classic, "Super Freak," the woman walked over to Mr. Lucky's table, placed one of her hands between his legs and asked him if would dance with her. She wasn't very attractive; in fact, she was a little chunky. On a typical Friday or Saturday night, he would not notice her. She was clearly not the type of woman he usually pursued. Since none of his buddies was in the club to tease him, he accepted her invitation to dance. After the dance, she joined him at his table, where she continued to fondle his groin. The two left the club about ten. The woman agreed to follow Mr. Lucky to his place, where they spent the night together.

When Mr. Lucky asked what had prompted her to make such a bold move on him at the club, she explained that she had been in town visiting a girlfriend for the past ten days. She had noticed him the previous weekend, when she and her girlfriend were at the club. She did not approach him, however, because he seemed to be busy talking to and dancing with other women. She further explained that she and her girlfriend were at the club again the previous Friday and Saturday nights hoping Mr. Lucky would be there. He wasn't, but her girlfriend told her that he was a regular, so she had come into the club by herself Sunday night, hoping to meet him before she left town. She successfully seduced Mr. Lucky by bypassing the head above his neck and boldly introducing herself to the head below his waist.

Rule of Thumb . . .

A man will quickly forget his perferences if he has an opportunity to sleep with a woman.

Handsome men, physically well-built men, men who have money, and celebrities all know that they attract attention in clubs. These men have larger egos and higher standards. Generally, they seek attention only from the most attractive women. These men also tend to possess an insatiable desire for a variety of women. The ultimate success for them is to leave a club with two women for a ménage à trois. A variation of the classic one man, two women ménage à trois may involve two men and one woman. My friend, Tony, refers to men who have experienced a ménage à trois after leaving a club or bar as members of *The Big Nuts Club!*

The Narcissist

Men who are narcissistic are usually comfortable in the club and bar environment!

The word "narcissist" comes from Greek mythology involving the story of a boy named Narcissus who fell in love with his own reflection in a pond. The popular definition of a narcissist is a person who is in love with himself. Contrary to his reputation, he is not really in love with himself in the true sense, but actually is in love with his own reflection. Studies indicate that his self-image was likely irreparably damaged by his parents' behavior, and his childhood relationships were often troubled. As an adult, if he finds himself getting too close to someone emotionally, he will fear abandonment and be prone to distance himself from or terminate a relationship. In so doing, he brings about the very abandonment that he feared.

The narcissist responds to those people who reinforce the image he has of himself. He wants and needs people to admire and applaud him and doesn't mind at all if some even detest him. He wants assurance that he is important. The respect and admiration of others is often more important to him than their love. People who do not reflect the image that he has of himself have no right to waste his time and energy. A narcissist is able to predict the outcome of his relationships with other people. He is fully aware of the price he will pay for being the way he is, but he can't help it!

A narcissist is easy to recognize.

- He is likely to be successful in his chosen career or profession.
- He doesn't require companionship.
- He is impatient, compulsive, and can be controlling.
- He doesn't accept criticism well.
- His behavior is often unpredictable; his moods change often.
- He is capable of turning against, punishing, or defeating anyone who threatens his self-image.

- He will alienate others and distance himself from relationships that he feels will be emotionally devastating.
- He feels a constant need to prove himself.
- He lacks empathy and doesn't identify with other people's needs and emotions.
- He believes that others envy him.
- He is sometimes arrogant and haughty.
- He has great imagination.
- He is cynical and judgmental.
- He abhors others whom he considers useless.
- He doesn't like to follow rules; he likes to make his own rules.
- He is always aware of the image he tries so hard to portray to others.
- He likes to do things on a grand scale.
- He is very protective of his time. For instance, he likes to screen his telephone calls.
- He will exploit people to confirm his grandiose self-image.
- He is dramatic in trying to influence others to think as he does.

So, why would a woman invest her attention, time, and energy with a narcissist? For the right woman, he is worth it! Since he craves love and admiration, he can cater to a woman's needs and desires in order to elevate his self-image.

The narcissist enters into a relationship with a woman cautiously. If he has been hurt in such a relationship before, he will be less likely to trust someone again. If he is sexually attracted to a woman he meets in a club or bar, he must feel there is compatibility between them before he will have intercourse with her. If she becomes a true reflection of him, a relationship can easily develop. It may be short-lived or may last a reasonable amount of time. The narcissist will terminate a relationship when he feels the emotional differences are too great.

The secret to dealing with a narcissist is to mirror his ego-inflating actions and get on his level. When faced with a mirror image of himself, the narcissist will generally retreat because he fears abandonment. By establishing a position of strength with him, he will fear being abandoned and will often change his behavior. Don't tolerate his whims and unreasonable desires.

The Biggest Turnoffs for Men

- Women who perform a head-to-foot, ten-point examination and financial analysis before deciding if they are going to accept an invitation to dance.

- Large or unattractive women who are dressed too provocatively. They might turn men on for a little while, but *Ms. Thang in the Booty Strang* is not likely to be approached by the A-list men in a club.

- Women who rudely turn down an invitation to dance. If you are not interested, refuse the invitation the same way you would want to be refused if you were asking a man to dance. Be clear but polite.

- Women who ask a man to buy them drinks. If a man is interested in you, he will usually offer.

- Rejections from women who are wearing press-on nails and have a $6-an-hour job.

- Women who pretend they don't know a man, after they have gone to bed with him.

- Single mothers who spend more time in the clubs than they do with their children.

- Women who pretend to be interested in a man they are talking to while looking at other men in the club.

- Women who deliberately put themselves in a man's way when he doesn't appear to be interested in them.

- Women who draw too much attention from other men.

- Women who have slept with several other men who occasionally or frequently visit the club.

- Women who dance without shoes.

- Chatty Cathys—These are women who want to tell a man their whole life story and reveal too much information about themselves the first night they meet him.

- Cinderellas—These are women who go to the clubs almost every night and rush to get home before midnight, so they can go to work the next day.

- Women who travel in packs. Men are hesitant to approach a woman in a group because they might be rejected in front of the group. Ladies, if you go out with a girlfriend or a group and you want to meet a man, you should occasionally separate yourself from the group so that you are more approachable.

Chapter 3

How Women Think in Clubs and Bars

Meeting men in clubs and bars is usually a ***choice*** for women. A girlfriend once told me that every woman in a club could go home with a man if she wanted to. Since women do have more choices, they can afford to have higher standards than men. Because women also have the natural assets and seductive skills to appeal to men's egos and libidos, they know how to play the games in clubs and bars better than men do.

Men would like to believe that women go to clubs and bars for the same reason they do—to meet someone. When women do go to a club or bar, it is usually based on one or more of the following reasons:

- They enjoy dancing.
- They are meeting a date.
- They are meeting a girlfriend to hang out with and talk to.
- They want to have a couple of drinks to relax and then go home alone.
- They are having a girls' night out.

- They are looking for a sugar daddy.
- They want to get drunk.
- They *are* looking for a sexual partner for the night.
- They are recently separated, divorced, or out of a serious relationship and want to get back into circulation.
- They want to meet a normal man with a personality.

I have found four things to be true about women in clubs and bars. First, they want attention from men. Second, they want to flirt with men. Third, they want sex as much as men do. There is a catch, however. Women want these things with and from the right men, and at the *right time!* The fourth, and most important thing about women is: *they follow their emotions.*

Rule of Thumb . . .

If a man stirs a woman's emotions, she will respond naturally.

Experienced women who are comfortable with the environment will usually go to clubs and bars alone. In experienced women, or those who want to discourage men from hitting on them, usually go with one or more girlfriends.

Sometimes, large women will go to a club or bar with a smaller woman, who will serve as bait. When men approach the smaller woman, the larger women will have an opportunity to attract some attention they might not otherwise receive if they were there alone.

There are four things women generally dislike about the club scene and only one thing they truly like. First, they dislike dressing up to go to a club or bar for a reason that will surprise many men. Second, they dislike not receiving as much attention from men as other women in the club. Third, they dislike that the club and bar scene always seems the same, with men still behaving as they always have. Finally, they dislike the smell of smoke in their hair and clothes. With so much they dislike, what could women possibly like about the club and bar scene?

Rule of Thumb . . .

A woman loves receiving the most attention of any woman in the club!

The competition between men in clubs and bars pales in comparison to the competition between women. Some women are more interested in making other women envious than they are in attracting men.

A group of regulars at our club often gather at the bar or a table and discuss various topics. One Friday night, we discussed how women dress in clubs and bars. One man asked, "What does a woman's manner and style of dress reveal about her mood or personality?"

Rule of Thumb . . .

Women don't dress to impress men in a club. They dress to impress and compete with other women!

There are two things a woman might wear to signal she is available: red high-heeled shoes may indicate a woman is interested in sex. White pantyhose might mean that she is sexually frustrated.

How Women Handle Rejection

Although women typically reject men more often than men reject women, sometimes a man rejects a woman because:

- She is too aggressive.
- He thinks he can attract a better woman before the night is over.
- He has his eye on another woman.
- He assumes the woman is being flirtatious to attract attention and really isn't serious.
- He is involved with another woman who may come into the club.
- An ex-girlfriend of his is in the club, and he is uncomfortable.

- He is looking for a one-night stand and doesn't believe the woman who has approached him is a candidate.
- He thinks the woman is looking for a one-night stand, and he is not interested.
- He suspects she is just looking for a man to buy her drinks.
- She doesn't meet his minimum standards.

Rejection is actually worse for a woman than it is for a man. One night, I had not been in a club more than a few minutes when a woman who was sitting at a table with a girlfriend stopped me as I walked by. She said she was glad a man had come in who looked as if he wanted to dance, and she asked if I would dance with her a little later. My response was, "Sure." I was not attracted to her, so I walked to the other side of the club to talk to some friends. A little later, the woman walked over to where I was standing and asked me if I was ready to dance. The dance floor was completely empty, and I really did not like the particular song the deejay was playing. When I responded by saying I really didn't want to dance, she asked, "Do you know how bad it is going to look for me to walk all the way back to my table after being turned down for a dance?" I offered to walk her back to her table, which I did. She was so appreciative that I had helped her keep her dignity that she bought me a drink. I did dance with her later—but only once!

When a woman is rejected by a man, she feels she is totally undesirable and unworthy of being able to compete with other women. Unless a woman who approaches you is ugly or just too aggressive, it always is a good idea to dance with her once, even if you have no interest in her. This lets other women know that you are approachable.

Another form of rejection can occur after meeting a man in a club or bar. Let's say a woman meets a man who appears to be her type. They talk, drink, and dance. He appears to be very interested in her. They exchange telephone numbers, but he never calls. The woman is perplexed. She might even call him after a few days have passed. When they do speak on the telephone, he says something like, "Well, I've been thinking that it probably is not a good idea for me to date a woman I met at the club I go to every weekend. It could cause problems since I know a lot of people there." If a man tries to explain why he hasn't called by saying "I've been thinking," he is telling you the truth. He has been thinking! He won't tell you, however, what he really thinks. He may feel that "I couldn't get you to go home with me the night we met, and you aren't as attractive as you were when I was drinking or when it was ten minutes until closing time."

Other than the fact that he may have been looking for a one-night stand, there are four other reasons a man may lose interest in a woman after he has met her in a club or bar:

1. He may be involved with someone else or he may be married.

2. He is not in the market for a relationship and thinks she is.

3. He is not really as interested in the woman as much as he is interested in the hunt and boosting his ego.

4. She may be GU, *geographically undesirable,* meaning she lives too far away for him to want to date her.

A Woman's Best Line of Defense

The most effective way a woman can discourage men from pursuing her in a club or bar is to display what is known as the *bitch shield.* When used effectively, the bitch shield deflates the male ego and usually stops a man dead in his tracks.

Let's say a man asks you to dance, and you are not interested. If you respond by still leaving him hopeful, he will likely approach you to dance later. If, however, you respond by shaking your head in a negative fashion while avoiding any eye contact, he will usually walk away and utter "bitch" to himself. If, for some reason, he continues to approach you, accept a dance from another man with whom you feel more comfortable. The first man will no doubt think you are a bitch!

This defense removes a man's hope by wounding but not killing him. A woman should never verbally attack or personally criticize a man she doesn't know, unless he is extremely rude, disrespectful, or too pushy. Responding to a request to dance by saying, "I don't dance with men shorter than I am," for instance, is too harsh and will be taken as a personal attack.

If you want to discourage a man who offers to buy you a drink, simply respond by shaking your head negatively. If he wants to know why you are rejecting him, tell him you prefer to buy your own drinks, and leave it at that. If a man you do not know has a bartender or waitress deliver a drink to you, have the bartender or waitress tell him that you prefer to buy your own drinks. An even better line of defense is to tell your bartender or waitress before hand that you do not accept drinks that are purchased by men in the club.

Rule of Thumb . . .

The bitch shield cannot be instantly penetrated or removed. In some cases, however, it can be slowly lowered until the woman is less defensive and more comfortable.

The High-Maintenance Woman

A high-maintenance woman usually has money and the attitude to go with it! Most likely, she has lived a charmed life. She may be an only child, the only daughter of wealthy parents, a *kept* woman, or a woman who is divorced from a very wealthy man. She is accustomed to being pampered, having the best that money can buy, and having her own way.

The financial security that money provides and the emotional security that being pampered provides often mask some inner insecurities. She has a greater need for attention than most women do. Here are some signs that a woman may be high-maintenance:

- She is vain.
- She wears designer clothing.
- She has fought the aging process with facial or body enhancements.
- She requires frequent confirmation that she is attractive and desirable.
- She lives alone in a home, expensive apartment, or condo.
- She either has no children or her children are grown and on their own.
- She has traveled a lot.
- She drives a sports car or luxury automobile.
- She generally dates younger men.
- She likes to do brunch on Sundays.
- She loves fine dining.

A high-maintenance woman usually seeks a man she can fix emotionally or financially. She wants a lot of attention, but in return will spend a lot of time and money on a man she is interested in.

Rule of Thumb . . .

A high-maintenance woman is prone to publicly displaying bouts of jealousy.

The Meetings in the Ladies' Room

One Friday night, Jesse, David, and I were at the club together. We were dressed to impress. As the crowd began to gather, two sisters, who were also regulars, came over to speak to us. After returning from a trip to the ladies' room, they said that three other women in the ladies' room had talked about us. They also told us that two other women in there were talking about the penis size of certain men who were in the club. They were speculating as to whether certain men were packing .22-caliber pistols, .45-caliber automatics, or 357 Magnums!

Having piqued our interest in what they had overheard, they shared more information with us about what goes on in the ladies' room. They explained that besides being somewhere women go to powder their noses, the ladies' room is also a sanctuary for things women want to talk about *when men aren't around.* Their language is often explicit, naughty, and sometimes filthy! In the ladies' room, women will discuss which women are wearing the tackiest dresses, their strategies for getting men to buy them drinks, and who they might want to go home with or take home with them.

The ladies' room also serves as a *war room* for women who may want to be competitive. Let's say you are sitting with or talking to a woman you are interested in. Sooner or later, she will go to the ladies' room. Let's also say there is another woman in the club who does not want to see you with the particular woman you are with. The second woman will notice when the first woman goes to the ladies' room and will then go there also. While the two women are in the ladies' room, the second woman may question the first woman, or she might say something negative about you in an effort to dissuade the second woman from being with you. In some cases, a woman will return from the ladies' room with an attitude, and her date will be clueless.

If you regularly frequent a particular club or bar, periodically ask some of the women you know if they have heard any juicy conversations during a visit to the ladies' room. You might be surprised to learn that you are often talked about!

The Biggest Turnoffs for Women

- Men who are conceited. Ask them what they like, and their answer would be "I like me almost as much as I like *myself!*"

- Men who don't know the difference between confidence and arrogance.

- Egotistical men who are *a legend in their own mind* and think they are God's gift to women.
- Men who approach women who are dancing together or alone and begin dancing with them without asking first.
- Men who talk on their cellular phone while in the club.
- Men who lie.
- Men who are drunk.
- Men whose breath is *stanking from dranking* or smells as if they just ate a "doo-doo" sandwich! It is always a good idea to have a breath freshener. Peppermints are good. In addition to keeping your breath fresh, they also have a calming effect on the body.
- Men who hang around a woman who is not interested in them.
- Men who assume a woman is sexually interested because she dances with them or allows them to buy her a drink.
- Men who are too touchy.
- Men who wear more jewelry than they do.

- Men who compliment too often. Women love compliments, but a man who compliments too often will be suspected of having ulterior motives.

- Overweight men with big bellies.

- Men who draw unnecessary attention to themselves by showing off or being too boisterous.

- Men who don't look clean.

- Men who talk incessantly about themselves.

- Men who try to hit on too many women in the club. Besides looking like a desperate loser, these men make women who might be interested in them feel like second-class citizens.

- Men who order one drink and carry the glass around all night long.

- Men who don't tip.

- Men who stand near the ladies' room. Women generally consider these men to be *bottom feeders*.

Chapter 4

Ages and Stages of Men and Women

The age of the clientele is one reason men and women select a particular club. Depending on the club, its patrons will range in age from twenty-one to over fifty. To some extent, how men and women behave in clubs and bars is directly related to what they think is important in their lives. As men age, they are generally concerned with three things: sex, making money, and enjoying life. As women age, they are generally concerned with four issues: their looks and physical desirability, enjoying life, finding true love, and being provided for financially.

"Have libido, will travel," reads the card of a single man in his twenties! During this time in his life, a man is in his sexual prime. He gets excited easily; everything turns him on! Among his biggest concerns are the size of his penis, his number of female conquests, and premature ejaculation. He wants to feel he is good in bed, but he probably lacks more in his technique than he realizes. Women who choose men in this age group often do so because these men are almost always open to sex. Although they may not be monogamous, men in this age group tend to stay in even stressful relationships if the sex is good.

Money, or more accurately, the lack of it, is of considerable concern to a man at this stage of his life.

Rule of Thumb . . .

A man's general attitude and outlook on life is established at age twenty-eight.

When a man enters his thirties, his financial status is generally better, and his dating activities reflect this. His attitude toward romance and sex becomes more pragmatic.

Men are now open to sexual variation, breaking old sex habits, and learning how to be a better lover. They may continue to feel a need to sow their wild oats, but they now are able to do it with a little more style. They will be a bit more selective in their choice of women, and they will be less tolerant of relationships that are stressful.

The fortieth birthday is the most traumatic for a man and is an important rite of passage. He reflects on how well he has managed his money and accomplished his personal and professional goals. By now, he is probably firmly established in his career. He wants to save money, invest, pay his obligations, and then have some fun and just blow some money! Having fun and enjoying life become very important.

By age forty, a man is more concerned about the quality

of time he spends with a woman than he is about getting laid every weekend. As a man gets older, he becomes happier knowing he can please a woman in the bedroom. Men in this age group are more comfortable with their sexuality, and sex can be quite an adventure, especially for a younger woman.

An older man in an upscale club or bar who displays character, confidence, and a "GQ" appearance will be interesting to women. Women who choose these men usually do so because:

- Older men are wise about life.
- They generally have a more positive outlook on life.
- They usually can offer the type of financial security that women enjoy.
- They are more compassionate and understanding about women's problems and needs.
- They are generally more patient and interested in a woman's pleasure.

There is a big difference between a woman telling her girlfriends that she has met *a man who is forty-five and a forty-five-year-old man!* A man who is forty-five will be described as a mature man, who looks and acts much younger than his years. A forty-five-year-old man will be described as a man who looks sixty!

In the "old days," a single woman was considered an old maid if she was not married before she was twenty-five years old. Today's single woman, however, is waiting longer to settle down. She thinks and acts differently from her older counterparts. She generally has not faced some of the issues an older woman has (e.g., marriage, childbirth, raising children, divorce, etc.).

There are two groups of twenty-something women. The twenty-one to twenty-five age group regards the early twenties as a time to explore and enjoy life, including low-commitment relationships. As women approach their mid to late twenties, they think a man's character and his potential as a possible mate are more important.

Women in their early twenties are easy to recognize in clubs and bars but are probably the most difficult to approach. They are usually with a group of male and female peers. Their agenda is to hang out together, dance, drink, and have as much fun as they can. Men of all ages will attempt to hit on these young women, often making fools of themselves in the process. Most twenty-one to twenty-five-year-old women are not interested in meeting a man in a club or bar and are quick to put up their bitch shields. Don't expect attractive women in their early twenties to approach men in a club or bar. They don't have to! They get all the attention they want. A man's looks rate high on the list of women in their early twenties.

There are two things that can work in a man's favor with twenty-something women. First, most women in this age group have not had many lovers, certainly not many good lovers, so their view of sex is only as good as the man or men they have been involved with. Second, these women either have low-paying hourly jobs or are just starting out in their careers. If they are accustomed to dating men of similar age, they probably have not had much money spent on them.

Twenty-something women are most likely to respond to handsome men who are slightly conceited and to men who appeal to their yearning for adventure.

Rule of Thumb . . .

The biggest secret to appealing to women in this age group is to make them think they want you more than you want them.

The thirtieth birthday is usually the most traumatic birthday for a woman. If she has never married, she may be concerned about the ticking of her biological clock and finding a husband. At this age, she also begins to be more concerned with how she looks and that she won't be as desirable to men as she was when she was in her twenties.

If a woman in this age group has been single for a few years, she probably has dealt with the club and bar scene and the games that go on there. If she is divorced, she may also be a single mother who has the responsibility of raising a child or children. As she is now older, she may seek the company of a man who considers her to be attractive, sexy, and desirable.

Since a woman in her thirties is likely to have a career, she tends to seek a man who is also stable in his career and financially secure enough for them to do things together that require money.

The forties can be a wonderful time for a woman to have fun, travel, and share unique adventures with friends and lovers. Unlike their younger counterparts, women in this age group know what they want and usually know how to get it. Usually, they don't have a problem approaching men in clubs and bars. At this stage of their lives, they have learned to be selective in their choice of men. They are wiser and much more relaxed about life and about relationships. They usually seek intelligent men with character, who can be their intellectual equal.

While most men reach their sexual peak when they are in their twenties, woman often reach their peak during their forties. Physical changes occur in a woman's body at this stage of her life, as she experiences menopause. With the gradual reduction of her body's level of estrogen, her vaginal walls will become thinner, and vaginal lubrication may decrease. After experiencing this change, however, many women enjoy a new and unique sexuality. They are often able to have better sex, since they no longer fear the risk of getting pregnant.

Girlfriends are more important to a single woman in her forties than they were when she was younger. A forty-something woman will likely have two or three close girlfriends and one super girlfriend. If the girlfriends like you, anything could happen in the spirit of fun and adventure!

Chapter 5

What Do Women Notice and Remember about Men?

When a man notices a woman in a club or bar, two thoughts immediately cross his mind: what she would look like naked and what she would be like in bed. Men notice contours and curves. Once we notice a woman, our imagination takes over. In most cases, it does not matter what she is wearing. For men, *imagination* creates *anticipation* and the hope of *participation!* This is the reason topless dancers are fully dressed when they perform their first stage dance.

Contrary to popular belief, women are more visual than men. While men *look more,* women are more perceptive and actually *see more!* They are conditioned to be able to see what they want to see, without staring or being obvious. A female bartender friend says, "Men *admire*; women *inspect.* A woman may already have decided she is interested in a man before she has caught his eye or gotten his attention!" Women notice form and structure. They also notice the eyes, hands, teeth, smile, and class.

Athletes and men with square shoulders, flat stomachs, chiseled chests, bulging biceps, and protruding buttocks represent three things that all women like in a man:

1. They are strong.

2. They are willing to work hard.

3. Most importantly, they have stamina or staying power.

When a woman notices a man, rarely are her initial thoughts sexual in nature. She is more likely to notice him because he looks like a man who can take care of himself physically, emotionally, and financially. He looks like he can handle most of life's challenges. Carla puts it a little more directly. She says, "A woman will notice a man who looks like he has a job; who looks like he has a good job; and who looks like he can hold a good job long enough to take care of her!"

There is a big difference between a woman who is interested in meeting a good man who happens to be financially secure and a woman who is a gold digger. Popular nightspots have their share of gold diggers—women who are not as interested in a man's emotional or physical fitness as they are in his fiscal fitness. Some women think that a man doesn't have to be much, if he has much!

Women are creatures of habit when it comes to the type of man they notice. A woman will instinctively take a second look at the type of man she is most familiar with or has fantasized about. A particular woman's type may include men who remind her of her father, men who resemble or act like a past boyfriend or lover, or men who fit her fantasy of her

Prince Charming. If a woman approaches a man for conversation or to dance, she usually does so because the man falls into one or more of these categories.

Rule of Thumb . . .

At one time or another, all women fantasize about being swept off their feet by their proverbial Prince Charming. Older women tend to fantasize more than younger women.

Women use their eyes to communicate their interest in a man. They apply makeup to make their eyes look larger and to draw attention to them. Men, on the other hand, will usually avoid eye contact with a woman they are interested in. Men will look up, down, and all around. They will notice a woman's hair, her face, and her body, but looking into her eyes is not a natural way for men to communicate their interest, attraction, or feelings for a woman.

Desmond Morris, artist and internationally established best-selling author of books on both human and animal behavior, has written about two changes that occur in someone's eyes when he/she is attracted to another person. First, the pupils expand. Second, there is a tear secretion that covers the entire eye. Dilated pupils and the additional tearlike glaze give the eyes an inviting, sexy, and dreamy look that makes us more attractive to the opposite sex.

A man's pupils will dilate when he sees a woman who

attracts him. If he looks into her eyes while his pupils are dilated, three things happen if she is also attracted to him. First, she will appear more attractive to him. Second, she will see the attraction in his eyes. Her pupils will also dilate, and a tear secretion will occur. Third, he will appear more attractive to her. A tear secretion then occurs in his eyes also.

The effect that our dilated pupils and tear-glazed eyes have on each other is most obvious in dimly lit settings. One reason dinner by candlelight is considered romantic is because light from a candle in a dimly lit room or restaurant causes the pupils to dilate and tear secretion to occur. Alcohol, especially wine, facilitates dilation of the pupils and tear secretion. In clubs, the combination of dim lights, the flashing colors of strobe lights, and alcohol makes it seem that men and women get better looking as the night progresses.

Although women say they don't like a man to stare at their bodies, they literally melt when a man they might be interested in looks deeply into their eyes. The man who knows how to use his eyes to convey his interest in a woman will be more successful than the man who avoids looking directly into a woman's eyes.

The importance of eye contact in a club should not be underestimated. Most men find it easier to talk, but in reality a man's eyes can communicate more to a woman than almost anything he can say. A normal feeling of guilt comes over a man when he looks into a woman's eyes, and she looks back at him. At this point, most men will look away and avoid direct eye contact. This is a major mistake! Exchanging eye contact is a critical stage of flirting and expressing your interest. By not returning eye contact, you lose what could be a tremendous advantage.

When a man looks deeply into the eyes of a woman, another interesting phenomenon can occur. His somewhat bold invasion of her privacy may become temporarily embarassing or intimidating for her. This is only slight, however, if she is interested in him. Mutual attraction often occurs quickly.

What is the most effective way to look at a woman in a club or bar? You want her to see a sexy gleam in your eye. Look directly into her eyes, and, as if you were going to hypnotize her, smile and think sincerely to yourself, "I like what I see!" Although flirting with a woman should not be an obvious come-on, there is nothing wrong in thinking of her sexually when looking into her eyes.

Using your eyes effectively with a woman has a twofold purpose. First, you express your obvious interest in her. Second, you can observe and read what she is communicating through her eye contact with you. Looking away after establishing eye contact with a woman implies weakness. When you establish eye contact with her for the first time, make her break the look! You may be uncomfortable, but try it; it works!

If a man uses his eyes incorrectly, he may destroy his chances of successfully approaching a woman. Women are intuitive; they can sense when a man is desperate or if he is confident, by the way he looks at them. If a man avoids eye contact, he sends a message that he lacks experience with women, is shy, or lacks confidence. If he stares too hard, he sends a message that he has ulterior motives. Men who aren't experienced with women look at them in a lustful way; men who are experienced with women look at them in a confident way that says, "I can have you!" This can be challenging to women.

Rule of Thumb . . .

Most women can tell if a man has cheating eyes, lying eyes, dishonest eyes, married eyes, wandering eyes, or sincere eyes.

Other than to see if he is wearing a wedding band, there are two other reasons women notice a man's hands. Some women equate the distance between the tip of a man's middle finger and the base of his hand, where the hand meets the wrist, with the length of his erect penis. Second, if a man's ring finger is longer than his index finger, purportedly, he has a high testosterone level. If his ring finger is equal to the length of his index finger, his testosterone level is average. If the ring finger is shorter than his index finger, his testosterone level is below average.

Women who are more interested in a man's qualities

notice men who are honest, outgoing, and confident, and who have style, intelligence, a sense of humor, and class.

Men who are outgoing are perceived as being likable, friendly, and genuinely interested in others. They develop and maintain a wide range of personal contacts.

Men don't smile as easily and as often as women do. Men are thinkers. Women are feelers, and if they are happy or experiencing feelings of joy, they smile.

Canvas a club on any Friday or Saturday night; you will notice very few men with smiles on their faces. Most of them look as if they really don't want to be there. I find this pretty amazing. I consider it an opportunity to get the edge on other men.

Rule of Thumb . . .

Average-looking people who smile often are more appealing than handsome men or beautiful women who don't smile.

A man's smile indicates that he is charming, optimistic, friendly, expressive with his feelings, likes what he sees, and most importantly, that he is approachable. When we smile, our facial muscles stimulate our nervous system to produce a hormone called *cerebral morphine.* This hormone gives us a pleasant, calming feeling. It also has an anesthetic effect. Notice men who are always with women in a club. I'll bet you ten to one they smile a lot!

Most men in a club are just guys, according to women, but some men are classy. How do women define a man with class? Renee responded to this question during a happy hour discussion by saying, “Class is like a rainbow. I don’t know exactly how to define it, but I know it when I see it. A man with class has an aura about him. He is articulate. He stands, walks, dresses, and carries himself in a way that just commands women’s attention.” A man with class does everything with style and a bit of flair. He is not ostentatious, however. He doesn’t have to turn on his class. He is as interested in other people as he is in himself. He is able to humble himself. Most importantly, he treats all women with class.

Rule of Thumb . . .

If a man wants women to notice him, he must give them something to notice other than that he is interested in sex.

A man will remember four things after meeting a woman in a club or bar:

1. If he slow-danced with her.
2. If he kissed her.
3. If he got her telephone number or e-mail address.
4. If he had sex with her the night he met her.

A woman will remember these same things as well after meeting a man. Women, however, also remember the following:

1. His initial approach.
2. What he was wearing.
3. If he was wearing a fragrance.
4. His choice of beverage.
5. If he was a gentleman.
6. If and how he interacted with other men and women.
7. If he made her laugh.
8. The first slow dance with him.
9. If she gave him her telephone number or e-mail address or if he gave her his.
10. The first kiss.

Rule of Thumb . . .

*A man remembers the things he **sees** and **accomplishes** when he meets a woman in a club or bar. A woman remembers the things she **sees, smells, hears,** and **feels.***

Chapter 6

Dogs, Players, Braggarts, and Liars

Men who have more fun "playing the game" in clubs and bars often reveal themselves to be dogs, players, braggarts, or liars. They are comfortable in the club and bar environment, and they are skilled at meeting women. This is not necessarily bad, as long as women recognize what these men want, and act accordingly.

Dogs pursue women solely for sex. They will not invest much time or money to do this. They don't give women an opportunity to pursue them because they are always the aggressors. A dog is fairly nondiscriminating and often pursues women who may not appeal to other men. By the same token, dogs offer little appeal to most women. They seek the lonely and sex-starved woman.

I once knew a married man who came to the local club almost every Friday night. He did not dress very well, but he always looked like he was having a good time. He became intimately acquainted with several women. Most of them, however, were women who did not interest other men. Mr. Bow Wow was honest. He always admitted that he was married and was only interested in sex. He concentrated on picking up women he called the "leftovers."

Dogs are confident, but they chase only what they think they can catch. They have a sense for spotting the "weak sheep in the herd." A dog's victims are usually women with low self-esteem, who believe the world consists of men who always prefer other women to them. Sex gives these women the chance to prove they are worth something, even if it's just being good in bed.

Women will tell other women that certain men in a club are dogs, unless they have slept with them. If a woman has slept with a man who turns out to be dog, she will not admit it. This would diminish her image. If a woman doesn't feel good about herself after sleeping with a dog, she may talk to her closest girlfriend. She will not, however, want other club regulars, especially other women, to know it took sex to get a man. Some say that dogs sleep only with other dogs!

Rule of Thumb . . .

A telltale sign that a man has a dog's mentality is if he casually refers to women as bitches.

A woman who gets emotionally involved with a dog can only blame herself when he doesn't return her feelings. He is only interested in sex. His approach and manner of pursuit usually provide enough clues for a woman to recognize his agenda. In clubs and bars, a dog's appearance can be deceiving. Big dogs, little dogs, mutts, pure breeds, mixed breeds, hound dogs, bird dogs, stud dogs, and the most evasive of them all, the show dogs, will approach women. Carla says, "Regardless of how a man looks, if he walks like a dog, talks like a dog, and acts like a dog, he is a dog!" Carla also offers some sound advice and a word of caution for dogs and their victims. "If you're going to get a piece of ass, treat it accordingly; don't mislead a woman. If you're going to be a piece of ass, treat it accordingly; don't expect a man with doglike qualities to get emotionally involved!"

Players *play* on women's emotions. By his very nature, a player is usually a consummate narcissist. He encourages women to become emotionally involved, but he is not interested in falling in love or even making a real commitment. He is usually good in bed, probably very good; he has had lots of practice. When other men refer to a man as a player, it is a compliment, a testimony to his ability to be successful with women.

Players are much more discriminating than dogs. They are usually seen with some of the most attractive women in a club. Women who become involved with a player will no doubt enjoy some romantic and fun times. Women must remember, however, that a player plays the numbers game to satisfy his ego. His success is measured not only by the number of women he is able to get into bed but also by knowing that he can get into a woman's head and her heart.

Rule of Thumb . . .

A player would rather attract women than pursue them.

A player will pursue women, but he wants women to pursue him. The reason is simple. If he has to pursue women, he operates from a position of weakness. He has little control. If women pursue him, he operates from a position of power. With power comes control. He knows what to do and when to do it. He also knows what not to do. He knows what to say and when to say it. He also knows what not to say.

In a club or bar, players usually carry themselves in a certain manner. There are ten signs and clues that women can look for that may indicate a man is a player:

1. He comes to the club by himself.
2. He dresses very well.
3. He drinks premium liquor.
4. He is smooth and articulate.
5. He is confident and sure of himself, but he is not overconfident.
6. He doesn't get nervous when a woman asks him questions.
7. He has not been in a serious relationship for some time.
8. He never looks at another woman while he is with you.

9. He appears to be financially secure.
10. He is more handsome than a woman thinks she deserves.

Although it is difficult to overlook these signs, a woman may not realize a man is a player until after she begins dating him. These are some additional signs to look for:

1. He never or rarely answers his telephone; he uses voice mail or caller ID to screen and pick up his calls.
2. His house or apartment is clean, well furnished, and color-coordinated.
3. He reads women's magazines.
4. He calls and leaves a message when he knows you aren't at home so that you will call him back.
5. He doesn't introduce you to his friends and family.
6. After you have slept with him, he acts like he can't quite place you or doesn't know you when he sees you.

The best way to deal with a player is to maintain control. Don't always be available for him. Give him the feeling that you are just a little out of his reach and that he must pursue you. If he tries to play on your emotions or control you in any way, think twice about getting involved with him!

Braggarts embellish the truth or tell harmless lies to prove they can run with the big dogs! They are usually insecure men who feel a need to over-promote themselves to meet women and compete with other men. If a man brags about what he does for a living, how much money he makes, mentions famous people he knows or is related to, or his education, he will also brag about his sexual exploits with women.

Rule of Thumb . . .

Shorter men tend to brag more than taller men do.

Women expect all men to lie from time to time. Some men will lie out of weakness, fear, or to boost their ego. In the club environment, men may lie to avoid an unpleasant situation. Chronic liars, however, are dangerous to everyone they meet because they generally have something to hide. They may be married, have criminal records, gamble, or be addicted to drugs. Chronic liars often betray others. They feel threatened, however, when they think they have been betrayed. More often than not, they also have a stalker's mentality.

Rule of Thumb . . .

The body doesn't tell lies; the ***mouth*** *does!*

If women know what to look for, a man's body movements will reveal when he is lying, according to body language experts. Women should carefully watch a man's eyes and hands, which often signal when he is lying. Liars find it difficult to maintain good eye contact when they are lying. If they do look at a woman when they are lying, their eyes will shift, and be unsteady. If a man talks with his hands, he will naturally spread his fingers apart while he gestures when he is telling the truth. If he holds his fingers close together, or keeps his hands closed while he is talking, he likely is lying. Remember, liars usually have something to hide. The most obvious clue a man is lying is if he places his left hand on his nose while he is talking. Many times liars will rub their index finger upward along the side of one nostril, then down the front of their nose.

A chronic liar's reputation will spread quickly in a club. He will continue his charades, however, until he has been caught in one too many lies. He usually then disappears from one club, finds another, and continues to lie his way into meeting new women.

Chapter 7

Bad Boys, Nice Guys, and A-List Men

Men often wonder why women seem to be more attracted to the bad boys than they are to the nice guys and good men who have the most to offer financially and emotionally. This is particularly puzzling since bad boys have the reputation of having little respect for women and treating them like a baby treats a diaper.

Very few women intentionally choose men who are going to treat them badly. Mother Nature has programmed women, however, to select the strongest, most dominant males to breed with. In the animal kingdom, males will often fight to win the favor of the female. The smaller and weaker males either leave the breeding area or get killed.

The bad boys' initial source of appeal lies in that they appear to be dominant males. They possess a combination of physical or mental toughness and attitude. They are cocky, and although they may be like players and dogs, one characteristic distinguishes them from other types of men.

As mentioned in the previous chapter, players are confident, poised, and selective. They would rather be pursued than pursue. They seek an emotional response from women, but they do not want to get involved emotionally themselves. Bad boys are also confident, but they project a "me Tarzan, you Jane" attitude. They usually dress down and may even wear athletic clothing. They will pursue women for sex, but women often pursue them. They don't want to get involved on an emotional level.

Bad boys will enter a club and immediately make the rounds to check out the women who are there. Although they display physical or mental toughness, they are not as aggressive as dogs. This lack of aggressiveness makes the bad boy mysterious and challenging to women. This is what distinguishes them from other men.

Rule of Thumb . . .

Women are often most interested in physically or emotionally rugged men who don't seem interested in them.

While the bad boys' initial appeal may be attributed to a simple law of nature, there are five reasons some women continually choose them over nice guys and good men:

1. They think nice guys are too meek and boring.
2. They don't think they are good enough for the "good men."

3. They are not interested in getting emotionally involved with a man.
4. They believe they can change a bad boy or expose a soft side beneath his tough exterior.
5. They are young and are thrilled to pursue a bad boy.

Women who choose bad boys over nice guys and A-list men are usually products of their past history. They are more adventurous, hardened, and more experienced than other women. They believe only physically and emotionally strong men can provide the adventure, thrill, excitement, and power they seek. Some of these women eventually tire of dating bad boys and learn to appreciate a nice guy or an A-list man. Most, however, continue to seek what they are accustomed to.

Sometimes women choose bad boys because they don't think they are good enough to date the nice guys or A-list men. Although they don't think they meet the standards of the good men, some women perceive themselves as being superior to the women the bad boys are accustomed to, and therefore, they *create* a challenge. This superior attitude can be a boost to a woman's self-esteem and give her the feeling that she can control a bad boy. This is wrong, however, because bad boys will eventually use this attitude against her, make her feel guilty, and humiliate her. Once a woman has dated bad boys, nice guys and A-list men will consider her emotionally damaged and will not be interested in her.

Women who do not want to get emotionally involved find

bad boys appealing, because they know these men are emotionally unavailable. These women may be recently divorced or recently out of a serious relationship. They are comfortable having sex without an emotional attachment. Ironically, bad boys may become emotionally involved, because they realize they are not in control and suddenly find themselves wanting something they can't have. In some cases, their emotions can turn into a dangerous obsession.

Bad boys also present a challenge for women who believe they can change them or expose a soft side beneath their tough exteriors. Women are attracted to men who are tough and tender. Like all men, bad boys may fall in love, change their ways, and become good mates for the right woman. The right woman, however, must be emotionally secure and patient. She must also be smart enough to understand that it is a man's nature to resist a woman's overt attempts to change him. Bad boys have habits that are particularly difficult to change. Carla compares a bad boy to a wild dog that has spent his life outdoors. "You can't bring a wild dog into the house and expect it not to shit on the carpet!" Neither the wild dog nor the bad boy is likely to change his habits if *forced* to do so. They will usually become vicious and turn on the person trying to change them. Change must be gradual and accompanied by benefits and rewards.

Younger women may be thrilled to pursue a bad boy because it provides a sense of adventure, danger, and conquest. Younger women, however, often don't know the difference between healthy and unhealthy relationships. To them, dating is a game. These women are willing to play the game for the opportunity to claim victory when they eventually dump one bad boy for the next one. These women know that bad boys like to be the *dumper,* not the *dumpee.*

Rule of Thumb . . .

Every bad boy likely has been dumped or had his heart broken by a younger woman at some time in his life.

Nice guys generally don't do well in clubs and bars. They are often overlooked and undervalued. Although they have many qualities women want in a man, they lack two qualities that are important to women. First, they do not appear to be confident. After they have had a couple of drinks to build their confidence, they might approach a woman and ask her to dance. If they are turned down, they are ruined for the night. Second, women do not find nice guys very challenging. Generally, they are too eager to please. Women will therefore conclude that they are meek and timid. Women also feel such men are boring.

Rule of Thumb . . .

Women appreciate courtesy, but in a club or bar, they are usually attracted to men who they perceive are manly and sexy.

A-list men generally aren't as aggressive as the men who are looking for a night's worth of fun. A-list men are observant and selective. They are attracted to women who radiate femininity and class. They are seldomly interested in women who are promiscuous, appear to be too experienced, or draw excessive attention to themselves. A-list men generally intimidate women with low self-esteem.

A woman cannot know if a man is truly an A-list man until she gets to know him outside the club. The obvious question then is what should a woman look for to know if a man is an A-list man? Here are some clues:

- He is intelligent and optimistic.
- He is neat in his appearance.
- He communicates well.
- He is not ostentatious and does not draw a lot of attention to himself.
- He is passionate about something other than his career, sports, or downloading pornography from the Internet.
- He is as *interesting* as he is *interested.*
- He is as *exciting* as he is *excited.*
- He looks at a woman he is interested in with a gleam in his eyes.
- He displays a sense of humor.
- He is courteous and friendly toward other men and women in the club.

- He is just a tad shy when he first meets a woman. A little shyness or nervousness appeals to a woman and lets her know that a man is not a dog or a player.

Rule of Thumb . . .

Men who approach women easily in clubs will likely discard them just as easily.

An A-list man is someone a woman would consider to be *relationship material.* A-list men do not have to be tall, handsome, wealthy, or famous. A friend of a girlfriend of mine once met a man in a club. He was professional, articulate, always well dressed, and possessed almost all the qualities that made him relationship material. The only problem was that he was only a little over five feet tall. After dating for a couple of weeks, the woman admitted to her girlfriend, "He's getting taller every day!"

How to Learn More about the Men You Meet

By talking with a man in a club, a woman can learn a lot about him: his job or career, the types of books he reads, his favorite movies and television shows, and his hobbies. If a man says he hates his job, reads dark novels, enjoys science-fiction movies, and never misses a home game of his favorite sports team, she might have some doubts about him!

A man's views and attitudes about life, work, women, and relationships often reflect the relationship he has or had with his father. When talking with a man, ask him about his father. What he says can provide valuable clues about his personality, his values, his view of women and relationships, and his outlook on life.

Men who constantly talk about their father, for example, usually need to prove themselves and try to measure up to him. They have often failed in their work and in their relationships. They are also likely to be distrustful of people.

Men who talk about their father's philandering, cheating, or many marriages, do so because they don't want to emulate him. These men will likely be monogamous and loyal mates.

Men who rarely or never talk about their father may come from a dysfunctional family. They usually find it difficult to sustain long-term relationships.

Chapter 8

Pawns, Rooks, Knights, Bishops, Queens, and Kings

Jeudi, an accomplished chess player, and I often compare the club environment to a game of chess, which is played with pawns, rooks, bishops, knights, queens, and kings. When she goes to a club, she enters with the attitude that *the queen is on the board!*

In chess, the pawn is the plainest piece on the board and outnumbers the other pieces. It moves straight ahead, one square at a time—if its path is not blocked—and never moves backward. On its first move, it has the option of moving forward one or two squares. If a pawn advances all the way to the opposite end of the board, it can become a queen.

The queen is the most powerful piece on the board. She can move any number of squares in any direction—horizontal, vertical, or diagonal—if her path is not blocked.

The rook is the second most powerful piece. It can move any number of squares in a straight line, horizontally or vertically—if its path is not blocked—but it cannot jump another piece.

The bishop can move diagonally across any number of unoccupied squares of the same color.

The knight moves in a special way. It moves in the form of an "L," two squares horizontally or vertically and then makes a right-angle turn for one more square. The knight can jump over other pieces to get to its new position.

The king is the most important piece on the board, for he is the prize and the object of pursuit by most of the other pieces. He can move one square in any direction unless he is checkmated.

The club environment is like several simultaneous games of chess. Different areas of the club may be considered different chessboards. On each board, men and women behave and interact much like the pieces in a game of chess. Women will act as though they are pawns, rooks, or queens. Men are similar to pawns, rooks, knights, bishops, or kings. Vertical, horizontal, diagonal, and L-shaped moves can be observed and easily defined.

A *vertical* move occurs when a man or a woman directly approaches someone of the opposite sex who is alone. Examples include asking for a dance, offering to buy a drink, or simply initiating conversation. Vertical moves allow you to show interest in someone one step at a time.

A *horizontal* move occurs when a man or a woman initiates indirect contact with another person. An example of this type of move would be buying a drink for someone and having it delivered by a waitress or bartender. Another example would be having a mutual acquaintance or friend communicate your interest to a third party. In both examples, this move is made with the expectation that it will lead to some form of direct contact with the recipient.

A *diagonal* move occurs when a man attempts to initiate direct contact with a woman although she doesn't appear to be available at the time. Examples include slipping a telephone number or a written message to a woman who is on a date, or making quick verbal contact with her when she is alone for a few minutes. While diagonal moves are direct moves, they are clandestine and not intended to be noticed by the competition.

The *L-shaped* move of a knight occurs when a man initiates direct contact with a woman who doesn't appear to be available at the time. This move is unique because it is made in the presence of a man's competition. A man may want to rescue a woman he thinks is with someone she wants to get away from. If a man is strongly attracted to a woman who is with another man, he may want to go around his competition and attempt to appeal to the woman as being the proverbial knight in shining armor. A knight will only make his move if he is relatively sure he can succeed.

In a club, male and female pawns always outnumber the rooks, bishops, queens, and kings. Since they are limited in their movement, they only play on one board within a limited circle of people. Even so, they tend to be quickly eliminated by more skilled players.

Bishops can best be described as men who want to appeal to a woman, even though she is not available at the time. Bishops will try to play on more than one board.

Rooks are typically married men or women. They will make bold, sweeping moves to cover as much ground as they can, as long as there are no opposing players in their path. They are usually discreet and will not draw much attention to themselves. They will also attempt to play on several boards.

A queen doesn't have much in common with others in the club. She doesn't get too close mentally, physically, or emotionally to others, especially pawns.

Rule of Thumb . . .

Queen status is often a lonely position.

Only the most confident men will approach her. A king will recognize a queen immediately and will occasionally glance in her direction. Any interest he has in her will wane if she is drawing a lot of attention from other men.

If a female pawn is skillful enough to become a queen, she may become one for just one night or she may become a permanent queen, depending on how she handles herself.

Remember, a queen doesn't get too close to others. Unfortunately, this is most difficult for a female pawn who has become a queen, because she knows only how to think and act like a pawn. After all, she used to be one. This new queen may foolishly think the pawns in her court are on her side, but this is not true. Pawns don't have the ability to appreciate what the queen goes through to become what she is.

A pawn that has become a queen is on her own. Although she is a queen, she is not accustomed to her new role.

Rule of Thumb . . .
Skilled players can quickly take out a female pawn who has become a queen.

The new queen must remember that she may be in the territory of an existing queen, and the stakes are higher than when she was a pawn. The original queen may view the new queen as expendable. Skillful players may seduce the new queen for the sole purpose of sexual conquest. If the new queen is too aggressive or reckless in capturing the attention of other players, she needs to know what she is doing or an undeserving player may capture her. Once a pawn becomes a queen, her best chance of survival is to gain the respect and confidence of her peers and slowly advance forward or even move to another board, where she will be the only queen.

In every situation, in every location, a king is usually present. He is where he wants to be and only moves one space at a time—a deliberate move intended to avoid drama. He does not seduce, nor does he chase. He is the key figure, worthy of notice, worthy of protection, worthy of being the last and most significant member of the game. Everyone else is expendable. A king allows himself to be surrounded only by his own. He does not intermingle with those of lesser status. It's just not done! He does not seek to attack but can if required. He is totally unaffected by what the other kings are doing but does consider what causes their defeat. He feels more secure with a queen by his side and regrets when she is forced out into the playing field. He blends into the crowd and moves behind others in order for them to receive the effects of an attack. The goal for the king is single-minded survival. Those who are on his side recognize him easily. Women instinctively know who the kings are and notice them when they enter the club.

The king is the object of desire to those on the opposing side. He is the one who blends briefly and then sets himself apart from the other players. He knows what he wants, where he needs to be, and what his objective is. He never steps into any other role than the one he was born into. While other players will move to different boards to seek conquests, a king has no reason to leave his own board unless he is in trouble or feels threatened. If a king is forced to move from board to board and continues to be defeated, he will eventually lose his status. He may continue to look like a king, but he won't act like one.

Chapter 9

Ten Principles That Give a Man a Competitive Edge

Women place men in a club or bar in one of three categories: men who *make* things happen, men who *watch* things happen, and men who *wonder* what is happening and why it isn't happening for them! On any given night, good looks or good luck might enable a man to meet women. Over time, however, successful men rely neither on their looks nor on luck to meet women. They have a competitive edge that makes women *comfortable* and *curious*. Here are the ten principles that can give a man a competitive edge with women in clubs and bars:

1. Get to the club early.
2. Dress to impress.
3. Get to know the club's waitstaff.
4. Tip generously.
5. Look like you are having fun.
6. Avoid acting like most men.
7. Think like women think.

8. Be seen with women.
9. Display confidence.
10. Engage each of a woman's senses.

Get to the Club Before the Crowd

On weekends the largest percentage of men arrive at a club between 11:00 P.M. and 1:00 A.M. The largest percentage of attractive women, however, arrive between 9:00 P.M. and 10:00 P.M. If you want to meet attractive, classy women, you should arrive about 10:00 P.M. By arriving earlier than most men, you will be able to meet at least five types of women that you might not otherwise have an opportunity to meet:

1. Women who want to avoid being hit on by the late-night crowd of men.
2. Women who drive relatively long distances to get to their favorite club.
3. Women who go out on Friday nights but have to work on Saturdays.
4. Women who have hired babysitters for the evening.
5. Women who go out on Saturday nights but go to Sunday morning church service.

Dress to Impress, Not to Depress

Since clothes usually cover about 95 percent of a man's body, it is only reasonable to expect women to notice what men wear. Women's tastes in men's clothing vary with their taste in men. Rarely will a man go wrong if he dresses for the occasion and wears clothing that accentuates his physique and overall appearance.

One Friday night, I was at the club with two girlfriends, including one who was there to meet a blind date. When a short man wearing an oversized yellow and black designer jogging suit and tennis shoes entered the club an hour later than promised, we were shocked to realize he was our friend's blind date!

Rule of Thumb . . .
Dress to appeal to the type of women you want to attract.

Men who dress to appeal to the type of women they want to attract know that if they look good in their clothes, women will wonder what they would look like without them! When a man dresses well, he will feel better about approaching women because he will feel more attractive, and therefore be more self-assured.

Rule of Thumb . . .

It is always better for a man to overdress than underdress.

Recently divorced men generally do not dress as well as single men. They may not know what's fashionable, never knew what was fashionable, or simply do not care to dress their best. Learning the importance of dressing well to create a good first impression with women can be an eye-opening experience for these men.

Rule of Thumb . . .

Women dress men better than men dress themselves.

For almost fifteen years, I bought most of my clothes at a small, family-owned department store. Over the years, I got to know the owner, two of his sons who worked in the store, and most of the salespeople in the men's and women's departments. Johnny usually waited on me. He knew what I liked. Johnny would usually call me when a shipment of new suits, shirts, or neckties came in and give me a chance to see the new styles before they were marked and put on the racks.

Georgette was hired one year to manage the women's department. One Saturday afternoon, I went in to purchase a couple of sport shirts and neckties to wear on the weekend. Johnny introduced me to Georgette as a long-time customer. She asked me what I was shopping for. She asked us if we would allow her to pick out two shirts and some neckties for me. She promised she would select items that would appeal to women, or the store would let me return the items and refund my money. I accepted her offer. I received more compliments from women on those two shirts and neckties than I had received on all the other shirts and neckties I had purchased over the years. Nowadays, I do not hesitate to let a girlfriend go with me to shop for clothing. If I don't take someone with me, I always ask the opinions of female customers or salespeople in the store. Since men generally see colors differently than women do, never underestimate the value of a woman's opinion when selecting colors that look best on you. Clothing selected by women will get you more compliments. Compliments from women provide an excellent opportunity to initiate conversation.

Colors are not important to most men, but they are very important to women! They notice the colors men wear. The best colors for a man to wear will vary, based on the color of his eyes, skin, and hair. Colors should be selected that enhance at least two of these three parts of the body. A man with blonde hair and blue eyes, for instance, should not wear bright red, unless he is representing a human form of the American flag. His choice of colors should include those that bring out the color of his hair and his eyes. On the other hand, red may be an excellent color for a man with a light mocha complexion and light brown eyes. A man with a full head of gray hair should select colors that contrast with his hair. Colors that appeal to women are colors that complement, or sometimes contrast with, a man's eyes, skin, and hair.

There are five basic color groups: neutrals, soft pales, midtones, dark, and deep bright colors. The variety of colors available in clothing stores will vary with the seasons.

If you frequent a regular club, consider adopting a certain color combination as your signature. For many years, I have worn various combinations of black and white shirts, ties, suits, vests, and shoes as my signature style of dress. Women will notice the unique way a man wears a certain color combination.

Speaking of unique color combinations, black worn with tan, sandstone, or khaki in the fall and winter looks good on most men. Yellow worn with the same colors in the spring and summer is also a good combination for most men.

Shorter men have a more difficult time dressing to appeal to women than tall men. If a man is under 5 feet 9 inches tall, the following things will make him seem shorter than he really is:

- Bright colors
- Pleated pants
- Cuffs

- Double-breasted coats
- Plaids
- Horizontal line patterns
- Sharply contrasting jacket and pants combinations

Suspenders or braces, darker-colored suits and shirts, suits or jackets with vertical stripes make a man appear taller.

Rule of Thumb . . .

A man should pay attention to a woman who compliments him on something he is wearing. If he doesn't know the woman, the compliment may be her way of letting him know he appeals to her.

Body Fragrances

A man's choice of fragrance can be very important to a woman's sense of smell. Two of the most popular and effective romantic fragrances are jasmine and musk.

Jasmine comes from the white, night-blooming flower of several Asian shrubs and vines from the genus Jasminium. It is used in perfumes, candles, and commercial fragrances for the home, and is considered the greatest aromatic aphrodisiac of them all. Legend has it that Cleopatra placed jasmine in her hair to distract Mark Anthony during business meetings.

The smell of jasmine is uplifting, promotes positive feelings, and has a euphoric effect.

Musk is especially used in commercial fragrances. It is a greasy secretion that is produced in a glandular sac beneath the skin of the male musk deer's abdomen. The smell of musk closely resembles the smell of testosterone, the male sex hormone.

Body fragrances should be applied to those skin areas where your blood vessels are closest to the surface. These areas are known as *pulse points*. As your heart beats, the heat generated from the blood at these points enhances the impact of the fragrance.

Women are attracted to the smell of a good cologne or *parfum*. A fragrance that blends well with your body can have a luring, seductive, and hypnotic effect on women. A man should own at least three different fragrances. By investing in a little time to shop and experiment, you will learn that certain body fragrances are very good for nightlife. Some fragrances are only available as colognes. Some are available as after-shave, colognes, and *parfums*.

Aftershave is a hydroalcoholic solution with from 1 to 3 percent perfume oil intended to scent, cool, and soothe the skin after shaving. The fragrance from aftershave generally lasts from one to two hours.

Cologne or eau de cologne is the lightest form of fragrance for the body. It is worn more during the day than at night and is intended to last all day. It may be used lavishly to refresh the body after a bath or shower. There is usually no difference between cologne and eau de cologne. Both contain from 2 to 5 percent of fragrant oils. Colognes are made in America; *eaux de cologne are made in Europe.*

Eau de toilette, also known as toilet water, is next in strength, containing from 4 to 8 percent of fragrant oils. It is created with a lighter concentration of fragrant oils than *parfums* to make a more subtle impression. Toilet water should be worn during the day and also may be used as an overall body fragrance before applying *parfum* at night.

Eau de parfum, a long-lasting fragrance, is just below the concentration of *parfum. Eaux de parfum* contain from 8 to 15 percent of fragrant oils.

Parfum is the most concentrated form of fragrance oil for a man. *Parfums* contain from 15 to 30 percent of fragrant oils and are balanced with specially aged denatured ethyl and water. *Eaux de parfum* and *parfums* should be worn at night.

Rule of Thumb . . .

Fragrances will react differently on people's skin, depending on how dry or oily the skin is. When selecting a fragrance, wear it approximately ten to fifteen minutes before buying it.

For many years, scientists have researched a subtle aroma that is secreted by all animals and insects and which subconsciously sexually attracts mates of the same species. These natural aromas are called *pheromones*, derived from the Greek language and meaning "transfering or communicating excitement." Pheromones are believed to be the primary source of what we commonly call "animal magnetism." In recent years, the power of pheromones has been explored on television news shows and in newspapers, magazines, and medical journals.

Natural pheromones are secreted from a man's armpits. They are often destroyed, however, by the use of soaps, deodorants, and antiperspirants.

Scientists have isolated and synthesized two of the most powerful human pheromones: *androstenol* and *androstenone*. Experiments have concluded that women are subconsciously attracted to chairs sprayed with synthesized pheromones. One report revealed that synthesized pheromones have been used successfully in merchandise showrooms to attract women, generate excitement, and boost sales. When used by men, women will reportedly make eye contact, smile, approach, and even initiate conversation.

Products containing synthetic pheromones can be purchased in department stores, specialty stores, and on the Internet. They can be applied sparingly to the pulse points, like cologne or *parfum*. When mixed with a body fragrance, experiments have confirmed that men get positive results.

Get to Know the Waitstaff

One Saturday night, a buddy and I were at our local club. A female bartender friend of ours, who worked at the club, introduced us to her roommate, a flight attendant. The roommate often worked on weekends, which prevented her from coming to the club. I moved along to visit another group while my buddy and the bartender's roommate talked and danced. My buddy admitted to me that he was attracted to the flight attendant. He was too intimidated by her good looks, however, to make a move on her. Besides, she was the roommate of one of our friends. Pursuing her could be a conflict of interest. As the night progressed, he noticed the flight attendant was looking at him with interest. Around midnight, he asked her what she was thinking. Surprisingly, she said, "I am just trying to decide whether I want to take you home with me!" Our bartender friend had told her roommate good things about us.

Waitstaffs have to put up with too much drinking, rudeness, undertipping, and oversexed men and women. They appreciate good customers, and if you are a good customer who knows the club manager, the bartenders, the waitresses, the deejay, and the bouncers by name, they will look out for your interests in surprising ways. Take care of them; they will take care of you!

Just as bartenders and waitresses will take care of their best customers, some have a unique way of handling troublesome customers. A few drops of a particular brand of eye drops in an alcoholic beverage, for instance, will usually cause acute diarrhea in less than thirty minutes!

Tip Generously

For men and women whose pay is partly based on gratuities, TIPS is an acronym that means "To Insure Prompt Service." If you open a credit card tab for the drinks you will be ordering, it is always a good idea to tip your waitress or bartender in cash. This will do two things for you. First, you will receive better service than other men in the club. Second, you will likely receive better drinks! Tipping in cash also lets women in the club know you are a good tipper. Women like men who tip well.

Look Like You're Having Fun

Women can sense when a man is desperate. They also notice a man who looks like he is having fun, and isn't at the club to pick them up. Don't go to clubs and bars primarily to pick up women, get telephone numbers, or meet Ms. Right. Find other reasons to go such as dancing, meeting friends, or making friends with others who are most like you.

Your position in a club is important. Sitting alone at the bar or at a table for too long gives women the impression you are desperate. It is okay to sit for a little while, but you should also move around. Don't stand in the corner. By all means, don't stand near the women's restroom. One of the best places to stand is near the dance floor or the band. Get into the music a little bit, and let women see that you have rhythm.

All men who go to dance clubs should know how to dance. Dancing can be a wonderful aphrodisiac for women. It also gives a man an opportunity to express his sensuality one-on-one. Most women are more impressed with men who know how to move their feet and bodies to the rhythm of the music than they are with the athletes, the pretty men, and men who just want to talk and hit on them. Being out on the dance floor has another advantage for a man—it gives women a chance to notice him.

Asking a woman you do not know to slow-dance before you have fast-danced with her or before she has indicated an interest in you is risky. You can, however, improve your chances of a positive response by doing the following:

- Approach her from the front or the side, never from the back.

- Smile and say hi. Do not tell her your name because you obligate her to tell you her name, which she may not want or be ready to do.

- Extend your right hand and simply ask, "May I dance with you?" or "Would you like to dance?"

Once the two of you are on the dance floor together, she will naturally follow your lead, if you place the palm of your right hand in the small of her back.

Rule of Thumb . . .

Most women think that if a man can't dance, he won't be good in bed. Most men think the same thing about women, by the way.

Avoid Acting Like Other Men

Many years ago, I was a friend to twin sisters. Whenever I was not romantically involved with a woman, we would go to our favorite club and watch the crowd. One of the sisters gave me some advice that I found profound and have never forgotten. She said, "If you want to meet women in a club, don't do what the other men do!"

Women expect men to behave in a certain way in clubs and bars. They expect men to stare and hit on them. They expect men to ask for their telephone numbers. They expect men to try to get them drunk in hopes they can leave with them. The attention may be flattering to a point, but if women aren't interested in the men, they will become defensive. When this happens, they are unable to do what is natural for them: flirting and being seductive. Men who don't behave like other men stir women's curiosity. Curiosity creates interest.

Think Like Women Think

I was out one weeknight playing backgammon with one of my buddies at a local club, when I noticed a very attractive woman sitting alone at a table. I remembered a valuable lesson a girlfriend had taught me. I asked our waitress to deliver the next drink the woman ordered with the message that "the tall gentleman at the backgammon table wanted to buy this drink for you." Most men would have faced her when she received the drink. I sat with my back to her, however, and continued to play backgammon. After approximately ten minutes, I walked over to her table and asked her if the drink was satisfactory. She answered yes and thanked me. I then asked her if she was waiting for a date. She told me she worked for one of the airlines and was waiting on some male friends with whom she worked, but I was welcome to join her at her table if I'd like. We talked, danced, and exchanged telephone numbers before her friends showed up an hour later. I stayed long enough to meet her friends before rejoining my buddy to play backgammon. I intentionally left the club later that night without saying goodnight; however, I did plan to call her the next day. Surprisingly, she called me after mid night when she got home. During the conversation, I asked her why she was comfortable calling me so quickly. She answered by saying, "You were different from most men, and you didn't try to hit on me."

By thinking like women think, you reverse the roles, so

women are more curious about you than they think you are about them. Once you have aroused a woman's curiosity, you have her interest. After you have her interest, she will likely want to know more about you.

There are three secrets to thinking like a woman thinks:

1. Create a little mystery about yourself.

2. Appear to be a real catch.

3. Play a little hard to get.

The following story illustrates how women react to men who create mystery. Two men occasionally came into our local club together. One always wore what looked like silk pajamas, Italian loafers, and no socks. He also carried a rather large appointment book at all times. The second man acted like a bodyguard for the first man. Although the man in the pajamas was a little bizarre to most of us, he was rarely turned down when he asked women to dance. He actually was a pretty good dancer. I don't know if he ever used his appointment book in the club. He did prove the point, however, that creating an air of mystery can be a great attention-getter for men. If you can be a little unique and creative, everyone in the club will notice you. The beauty of getting attention is that several women will notice you.

This man's gimmick was a bit extreme. There are less ostentatious ways a man can create a little mystery about himself to incite women's natural curiosity. The secret is to create mystery without creating suspicion. Giving out a pager number for instance creates mystery, but it also creates suspicion.

One man I know is a master at creating mystery for women he meets by temporarily retreating after, and only after, he knows he has aroused some interest on their part. He doesn't retreat until he has ordered a fairly uncommon drink such as a dirty vodka martini on the rocks, established some eye contact, and engaged a woman in light conversation. During the conversation, he smiles, and usually compliments her once. When he does retreat, he moves around the club, chatting with the waitstaff, the deejay, and other men and women he knows. He never gives the impression, however, that he is trying to pick up other women. Every fifteen minutes or so, he will return to the woman he has met. He will ask her if she is having a good time. He may ask her if she is ready for another drink. He may ask her to dance. Between visits, he will attempt to establish more eye contact from another location in the club, but he does not stare. More often than not, one of three things eventually happens:

1. The woman will return and hold eye contact from across the room.
2. She will ask *him* to dance.
3. She will ask him if he would like to join her.

When men look back over their lives, they reflect upon their accomplishments. When women look back over their lives, however, they reflect upon their relationships. In order to be considered a real catch, men must gain a woman's emotional acceptance and be perceived as *relationship material*. This doesn't mean that all women in clubs and bars are looking for serious relationships. It simply means that women are curious about men who offer the prospect of romance, excitement, passion, sensuality, adventure, friendship, and devotion.

Women tend to discount men who frequently go to clubs and bars as relationship material. The reason is simple, according to Carla. "If a woman meets a man who spends a lot of time in the clubs, guess where he will be the first time they have an argument?"

Rule of Thumb . . .

Men who meet women primarily in clubs and bars are generally commitment-phobic and aren't willing to work to develop a serious relationship. This same rule of thumb applies to women.

Women will test a man's interest by playing hard to get. Most men move so fast that they don't take time to realize that this works both ways. By being a little evasive and unavailable, a man can get into a woman's head and make her believe she wants him more than he wants her. A woman is more likely to expend extra effort to get and keep a man's interest, if she thinks she cannot have him or that he may get away.

Men typically respond to what they think; women typically respond to what they feel. If a man is a little hard to get, a woman is forced to think about him. The more she thinks about him, the more she fantasizes about him. The more she fantasizes about him, the more she will want him.

Rule of Thumb . . .

You've got to get into a woman's head before you can get into her bed!

Be Seen with Women

Most men in a club are either shy, lack confidence, or fear rejection, so they wait, watch, and hope that a woman will approach them.

Rule of Thumb . . .

In the land of the blind, the man with one eye is king!

Successful men are outgoing and interact with a number of women, without giving the appearance they are hitting on them. Women are perceptive. Just as they can sense when a man is desperate, they also can sense when a man is experienced with women. This is not a bad thing. If women observe that you are friendly with other women, they will perceive you to be a man who is comfortable with himself and someone women are comfortable with. If you are generally friendly with women in a club, other women will notice.

Display Confidence

Self-confidence can tip the scales in a man's favor with women in a club. Women instinctively look for clues to a man's level of confidence. Confident men are usually relaxed and patient. They have a certain look and style in the way they carry themselves. A man who is confident radiates high self-esteem. High self-esteem generates sex appeal!

A technique for increasing your self-confidence is to perform a special gesture each time you are successful. The special gesture may be as simple as touching your mustache, putting your hands together, making a fist, or rubbing your chin for a moment. When a new opportunity presents itself, do this to remind yourself of your past successes. One buddy of mine does something a little different to give him extra confidence. He normally drinks Jack Daniel's and Coke. When he sees or meets a woman whom he is interested in, he switches to gin and orange juice. He explained to me one night, "When you see me drinking gin and juice, it's all about sex!"

Engage a Woman's Senses

The most erotic experiences for a woman involve all her senses. By engaging a woman's sense of sight, hearing, taste, smell, and touch, you also engage her sense of well-being, her intuitive sense about you as a man, and her sensuality.

Michael entered the club on Friday night about 9:30, wearing a black suit, a bold yellow and black necktie that a girlfriend had selected for him, and a yellow pocket silk. The club was not crowded yet. He noticed an attractive woman sitting at the bar. He watched her for a few minutes, noticing that she would occasionally look at her watch, as if she were waiting on someone. Michael walked up to the bar, stood to her right, and ordered a drink. He didn't order a common drink; he ordered a black martini. As he waited for the bartender to return his change, the woman curiously asked him what he was drinking. He told her it was a black martini, which is also known as a midnight martini. He then extended his glass to her to taste his drink, which she did. "I like that," she said. "I may have to order one for myself a little later." Michael then introduced himself. The woman responded by telling him that her name was Stephanie. As they shook hands, Michael purposely held her hand a little longer than normal. He asked her if she was waiting for someone. She told him that her sister was supposed to meet her at the club between 9:30 and 10:00.

As the two chatted, Stephanie commented that she really liked the necktie Michael was wearing. They continued to chat mostly about their professions for about thirty minutes until her sister arrived. Stephanie introduced Michael. He asked them if they would like to move to a table before the club became crowded. They agreed. Michael noticed that Stephanie's sister was moving to the fast beat of the music the deejay was playing, so he asked Stephanie if she would mind if he danced with her sister. "Of course not," she answered. When the two finished dancing, Michael walked Stephanie's sister back to the table and then went to the deejay booth. He asked the deejay, whom he knew, to play a particular slow song and tipped him five dollars. When the slow song began playing, Michael asked Stephanie if he could have the pleasure of dancing with her to one of his favorite songs. As they began to dance, Michael placed his right hand on Stephanie's lower back and held her right hand with his left. She could smell the fragrance he was wearing and asked him what it was. About halfway through the song, he released her hand and placed his arms around her waist. She responded by placing her arms over the top of his shoulders around his upper back. Michael did not make the mistake most men make when slow-dancing with a woman for the first time. He did not pull her into him. He allowed Stephanie to feel comfortable enough to move closer to him. As they finished the dance, he looked into her eyes and whispered into her ear, "I love the way you follow me!" She responded by whispering into his ear, "It is easy to follow you; you lead very well."

Rule of Thumb . . .

Most men are sexually aroused by their sense of sight. Most women, however, are more sexually aroused by their sense of hearing. Whispering can be a very sensual technique to communicate with a woman in the noisy atmosphere of a club.

When they returned to their table, Stephanie looked at Michael and asked if he would order her one of those black martinis. He ordered one for each of them. In fact, he bought drinks for Stephanie and her sister the rest of the night. Stephanie's sister danced with some of the other men in the club and had a good time. Stephanie's interest, however, was focused only on Michael. By engaging all of her senses, Michael had fully captured Stephanie's attention and interest. The two exchanged telephone numbers that night and dated for several months.

Chapter 10

If You Can Sell, You Can Meet Women

In the sales world, we have a saying, "Selling doesn't begin until somebody says NO!" Selling products or services to customers often requires selling over their objections. Selling yourself to women often requires selling against rejection. David has a definite salesman's philosophy when it comes to meeting women in clubs. "When I see a woman I would like to get to know, I have to modify her behavior toward me."

Successful salespeople possess four skills that set them apart from other salespeople:

1. They communicate well.
2. They make things happen.
3. They are creative.
4. They know how to arouse interest in their product, their service, or themselves.

Rule of Thumb . . .

Selling is not a science; it is a process.

A few years ago, I worked with one of the smartest young single male sales professionals I have known. Although he was an expert in giving presentations, gaining the trust and respect of his customers, and closing sales, he did not consider himself a ladies' man. In fact, he rarely dated. We often discussed the similarities between the *four-step process* used to secure sales and a similar *five-step process* for meeting women in clubs and bars. The four-step process for securing sales consists of prospecting, qualifying, presenting, and closing. The process for meeting women in clubs consists of *prospecting, qualifying, approaching, attracting*, and *closing.*

Somewhere along the way, my young friend incorporated the principles of selling into his personal life. He eventually met a beautiful waitress at a local club. They dated for two years and are now married.

Prospecting

The first step in meeting women in clubs is being alert to situations and recognizing opportunities and prospects. Some men enter a club like a kid in a candy store and immediately begin hitting on women, which is a sure recipe for failure. Women are observant. They notice men who try to hit on too many women, and they will usually avoid them.

One of my girlfriends recommends that men practice the *Fifteen-Minute Rule.* Spend the first fifteen minutes you are in a club observing and allowing yourself to be seen by the women there. Once you see a woman you want to dance with, ask her to dance. If she declines your invitation, you might ask a second woman to dance. If she also refuses, wait fifteen minutes before you approach another woman for a dance. If you attempt to talk with a woman, but she is non-receptive, wait fifteen minutes before you approach someone else. During the fifteen-minute periods, talk with the deejay, one of the waitstaff, or with one or more of the other men. Avoid seeming like you are desperate! However you try to be seen by women during the fifteen-minute intervals, my girlfriend advises that you don't get on the dance floor and dance solo unless you are a regular! If other men and women in the club do not know you, dancing by yourself on the dance floor gives the impression that you might be gay.

Some men are more successful prospecting when they are with a buddy. One year at our national sales meeting, some of the guys had a little too much to drink and began mooning the crowd during a hospitality gathering. Someone took instant photos of this behavior. Danny and Joe managed to get their hands on two of the photographs before they decided to leave and go dancing at a nearby club. When they entered the club, they noticed a group of women who were sitting at a table and who looked like they were having a lot of fun. Danny and Joe walked over to them and pulled out their wallets, where they had placed the mooning photos. They flipped them open and said, "We are with the FBI. Have you ladies seen either of these assholes?" While this approach might have been embarrassing for a single woman, the group of women thought this was so funny that they took turns dancing with them for the remainder of the evening.

If two buddies look like they are having fun in a club, they don't look desperate or give the impression that they are there to pick up women. Women are likely to view them as being more normal than other guys who prowl a club or stand in a far corner at the back of a club. They will likely be more receptive to having fun with buddies.

Rule of Thumb . . .

If you are with a buddy who is boisterous, discourteous, or desperate, separate yourself from him. If you don't, you will be guilty by association!

Qualifying

In sales, a single prospect may or may not be the right prospect to make a sale to. We often use the *spaghetti-on-the-wall technique* to qualify several prospective customers simultaneously. This technique suggests that if you reach into a vat of spaghetti, take out a handful, and throw it against the wall, most of it will fall to the floor, but some of it will stick.

In a club, a man will no doubt be interested in meeting women who may or may not be interested in meeting him. There are three methods a man can use to qualify prospects. The first is to approach a woman directly and then qualify her. This method requires a man to commit time and possibly risk rejection. The second method is to notice the women who are noticing you. The third and most effective way is to create interest. By creating interest in a way that is noninvading but comfortable for a woman, the process of qualifying is much simpler, and more effectively sets the stage for the next logical step, the approach.

Rule of Thumb . . .

*Men who pay attention to **several** women without hitting on them arouse interest from other women.*

A man who is attentive and respectful to all women is appealing. The more women a man pays attention to, the better his chances are of meeting one who will be interested in him. When women observe a man being attentive to other women but not hitting on them, they will consider him to be confident and able to interact with all kinds of people. Women appreciate a man who doesn't discriminate.

Notice the Women Who Are Noticing You

Sometimes, men in a club are so busy attempting to hit on women who aren't interested in them that they fail to notice those who are interested. Because women are not usually very obvious in showing their interest, successful men are always aware of women who might be noticing them, and they act accordingly. An old technique that has been practiced by women for years will illustrate the importance of noticing the women who are noticing you.

Let's say two girlfriends are in a club together. One has noticed you and is interested. She will take a strategic trip to the ladies' room by walking directly past you. She won't look at you or say anything, but as she walks by, the second girlfriend will observe your reaction to the first one. When the first girlfriend returns from the ladies' room, the two will discuss how you reacted to her. If you ever notice girlfriends doing this in a club, you will also notice that most men fail to recognize what is really happening. The man who is aware of this technique will wait until the first girlfriend returns from the ladies' room. If she walks past him, he will look at her and smile if he is interested. He may say something to her, or he may wait until she rejoins her girlfriend, after which he will go over and start talking with them.

Meeting as many women as you can without hitting on them allows you to quickly sharpen your skills and your ability to qualify potential prospects. Meeting as many women as you can is very similar to interviewing for a job—you get better the more you do it. Your confidence will increase, and you will develop a keener sense for qualifying prospects. Another advantage to doing this, even if you have no romantic or sexual interest in them, is that they may invite you to social gatherings outside the club as a friend. They may also have girlfriends they want you to meet!

Notice What a Woman Is Drinking

Professional bartenders remember people by what they usually drink. My bartender buddies all agree that a person's choice of alcoholic beverage usually reveals something about their personality and perhaps their agenda. This is especially true for women. As you observe and meet women in clubs and bars, notice if they are drinking any of the following:

- Chardonnay
- White zinfandel
- Beer in a bottle
- A mixed drink
  (e.g., rum and Coke, gin and tonic, 7 and 7, scotch and soda, etc.)
- A frozen drink (e.g., margarita or daiquiri)
- Long Island iced tea
- Shots

Chardonnay is the most popular wine in the United States. A woman who drinks chardonnay is likely a professional woman who is well traveled and financially secure. She is usually easy to approach, especially if the man is a well-groomed professional man. To be successful in meeting and talking with her, a man should keep the conversation at a high level and not come on too strong. She may be willing to exchange business cards with you. At the very least, you should give her one of your cards, and let her know you would enjoy the opportunity to see her again. You are not likely to convince her to go home with you the first night you meet. If she is interested in getting to know you, she will let you know in her own way.

White zinfandel is the second most popular wine in the United States. Women who drink this are more challenging because two different types of women drink "white zin." The first type knows a lot about wines. She is accustomed to drinking wine with her meals. White zinfandel is fermented without the skins of the zinfandel grape. Its semi-sweet and fruity aroma and taste can be enjoyed without a meal. She usually orders the best brand the club has in stock. Her taste in men is very similar to a woman who is drinking chardonnay.

The second type of woman who drinks the club's house white zinfandel knows very little, if anything, about wine. What she lacks in substance, she will attempt to make up for in style. The name alone, white zinfandel, sounds classy.

That is what this woman desires to be, a woman with class. She is usually interested in attracting a man who has something to offer her.

A woman who drinks beer out of a bottle is likely a "girl next door" type of woman. She has no expectations and no agendas. She is not as much into games as other women in the club may be. There is a good possibility that she will refuse if you ask her to dance. She may or may not enjoy dancing. She may think you are trying to hit on her. Her refusal may sound a little harsh, but remember, she usually has no expectations or agenda. She isn't pretentious. To be successful with her, you must give her an early indication that you are interesting and different from most of the men in the club, and that you also do not have an agenda. If she feels comfortable, she will likely relax and take the initiative to get to know more about you. Once she develops an interest, the evening will probably be fun for both of you. The key to being successful with her is to let her take the initiative.

A woman who drinks a mixed cocktail is generally sociable, easy to talk to, and comfortable with herself. This is particularly true if she is drinking premium liquor instead of well liquor. Well liquor is generally the least expensive house liquor and is what you will get if you do not call your liquor. Her choice of drink allows her to slowly wind down and begin to enjoy the crowd or the music. Rarely will this woman overindulge. If you are also drinking, she will offer to buy you a drink, if she is interested in you. To be successful with her, use lots of eye contact, engage in good conversation, and allow your sense of touch to work for you.

How do you characterize a woman who is drinking one of the *foo foo* drinks such as a frozen margarita or a daiquiri? My bartender friends tell me that these women are generally looking to have a good time but with no sex involved! They may dance very provocatively. They will tease you, and, of course, they will let you buy them more drinks, but unless they are the aggressors, your best moves will likely not get you very far.

At one time or another, we have offered to buy a woman a drink, only to have her order a Long Island iced tea, even if she had been drinking something else before. If a single, unescorted woman or a woman who is with a girlfriend orders this drink for you to pay for, she is probably looking for a man to finance her night out. She may get a nice buzz and allow you to do a slow grind with her on the dance floor, but don't expect to get to second base. She will entertain you just enough to keep the Long Island iced teas coming. Now, if a woman is buying this drink for herself, she has a different agenda. She definitely wants to get a quick buzz for one of several reasons. She may have recently broken up with a boyfriend. She may need to loosen up before she is confident enough to dance or approach a man she is interested in. If she is buying and you have an interest in her, stay close to her, and assure her that she is safe with you. She will do the rest.

Finally, let's look at the woman who is drinking shots as if they were going out of style. She may be wanting to drown herself in her sorrows. She may be celebrating something as good as a promotion or as bad as a divorce. She may just want to get drunk. Whatever her reasons, she could be the easiest prospect in the club for you. If she has a tendency to be a little suggestive or outright forward with sexual talk, time is on your side. The key to being successful with her is to buy a couple of rounds of shots for the two of you and encourage her to share her agenda with you through physical contact. This may occur if you are on the dance floor with her, or she may be bold enough to touch you in a suggestive way. The onus is on you to recognize when the time is right to suggest taking the party to your place or hers.

Rule of Thumb . . .

Women often drink their cocktails through straws to get a quicker buzz. Air taken in through a straw with a drink causes the alcohol to have a quicker effect.

Approaching Women

Approaching women in a club or bar is the most difficult, yet most critical, aspect of selling yourself and is where most men fail. These women are similar to customers in the business world. Sometimes a man has to make a cold approach to be successful.

A man's attitude often makes the difference in how a woman will react to his approach. Most men fear failure when they approach women in a club. This attitude generally results in a self-fulfilling prophecy. Successful men, however, approach women with a desire to succeed. They practice the five Cs:

1. They are *confident* but are not cocky.
2. They *communicate* well.
3. They are *creative.*
4. They arouse *curiosity.*
5. They make women feel *comfortable.*

Women remember men who are different in their approach. By doing something different, your objective should be to try to capture and hold her attention long enough for her to find you interesting and different from other men. If you don't give a woman a reason to be comfortable and curious, she will generally react only to your looks. A woman rarely remembers men who approach her in a common way unless they are handsome, famous, or wealthy. Ask her, however, if she remembers the men who approach her in a unique way and she will. It's okay to do something that takes a woman by surprise but doesn't embarrass or obligate her to do something.

An average-looking but well-dressed man walked over to Denise's table one Friday night, where she was sitting alone. He handed her a folded note and a pen, then walked away from her table, went to the bar, and wrote down a drink order for the bartender. Denise opened the note, which contained the following message: "Hi, unfortunately I have a mild case of laryngitis tonight. Although I am temporarily unable to talk, I can dance very well. If you would like to dance later, would you please let me know?"

After he received his drink, the gentleman looked in her direction. She was smiling, as she motioned with her index finger for him to come over. He walked back to her table and she handed him the folded note and pen. He opened the note. She had written: "I can't dance very well, but I can talk. I think we should dance." The gentleman escorted her to the dance floor. He was an excellent dancer! When they finished dancing, he walked Denise back to her table and said, "Thank you very much. You are a very good dancer." Shocked, she asked him why he had lied about having laryngitis. He explained that he noticed that she had turned down three other men who had asked her to dance before him. He knew he had to do something different to get her attention, so he wrote the notes for her and the bartender. They laughed. Denise complimented him on his creativity and then asked him if he would like to join her at her table, which he did.

When you see a woman you want to meet, walk over to her, but do not park yourself. Look at her, smile, say hi, and ask her the following question: “Are you waiting for someone, or would you be available to dance if I ask the deejay to play a good dance song?” If she indicates she would be interested in dancing, tell her that you are going to the deejay booth to request a song. You then tell her that you will give her a nod when your request is played. Be sure also to tell her that if the deejay plays a song that she likes before your request is played, to give you a nod. Request a song from the deejay. Be sure to tip him or her generously. Go back to where you were standing or sitting and wait.

This approach will accomplish four things for you:

1. You distinguish yourself by not pressuring the woman to give you an immediate answer.

2. You don’t indicate that you are hitting on her.

3. You give her an opportunity to loosen up and mentally prepare herself to get on the dance floor.

4. Most importantly, you provide the opportunity for her to initiate the first dance if she is interested.

One of my buddies, Gary, defines insanity as, "Doing the same thing the same way and expecting different results!” If you always approach women the same way and get the same negative results, change your approach!

Opening Lines—Do They Really Work?

It is almost impossible to read a book on meeting women that doesn't contain a chapter on great opening lines or pick-up lines. I am going to tell you something different. I believe women recognize canned opening lines for what they are, a fishing line with bait and a hook. A smart and savvy woman is not likely to take this bait! Unless she has lived under a turnip truck all her life, she has probably heard most of the opening lines or variations of them. They can be cute and clever but seldom are they original or sincere.

Rule of Thumb . . .

Women like originality and sincerity in a man.

One night when I was out at a club, I overheard a man ask a woman whom he had just met if she believed in the hereafter. When she answered yes, his reply was, "Then I guess you know what I'm in here after!" I had to give the guy an A+ for being so bold, but this line was an immediate turnoff for the woman. As I observed the man the rest of the night, he bounced from woman to woman. I surmised he was laying the lines down to all of them. From what I could see, he struck out with every woman he attempted to talk to. At one point, I noticed he tried to hit on one of the women I knew. I asked her if his approach was sincere, and sure enough, he had dropped one of those tired lines on her. Without even extending the courtesy of saying hi and introducing himself, he walked up to her and said, "Damn, baby, your ass is so fine, it's a shame you have to sit on it!"

There is a major difference between an opening line and an icebreaker. Opening lines sound prepared and rehearsed, because they usually are. Icebreakers provide an opportunity for you to be yourself and utilize a little creativity to begin a conversation with a woman. There are no magic icebreakers that apply to men universally. They must reflect your individuality and the environment you find yourself in. The most effective way to break the ice and put a woman at ease is to talk about something you both are interested in. If you don't know you have similar interests, consider asking her an open-ended question or ask her opinion about something. If all else fails, say something silly and watch her reaction, but be sincere. You will know if you need to shift gears and be more serious. Whatever you decide to say, just relax and be yourself.

Here are a couple of parting thoughts on this subject. When a man meets a woman, he is selling himself. The sales process involves prospecting, qualifying, presenting, and closing. There is no step in the selling process called opening! If opening lines are so great, why do men feel they have to have them and women don't? A woman is most likely to be herself, be direct, and tell you what is on her mind. Should men be any different? Instead of using rehearsed opening lines to put a woman at ease with you, try simple and sincere ice-breakers, let women know you are a good communicator, and concentrate on closing effectively.

Rule of Thumb . . .

Good verbal closing skills are much more effective than trite opening lines.

Breaking the Ice

Women tend to be thick-skinned in clubs and bars. Most of them know they are going to be hit on by the wrong men. Accordingly, they mentally prepare themselves before they enter a club.

Your first words often determine how quickly and how well you connect with a woman. Keep your initial conversation light and convey your interest in a safe manner, without coming on to her. Your conversation should not be overpowering. You should not talk too much about yourself. Your main objective should be to set yourself apart from the other men in the club and arouse the woman's interest. If you are too aggressive, a woman may resist your advances because you are like all the other men. Be generous but not overly generous with compliments. Concentrate on her interests, not yours. Listen more than you talk.

Asking open-ended, thought-provoking questions is a good way to begin talking with a woman. Women are more likely to respond to conversation initiated by a man than they are to start talking about themselves. When I have successfully engaged a woman in light conversation, I have had a lot of fun by asking the question, "What would be the first thing you would likely say if you accidentally hit your thumb with a hammer?" Most women will hesitate to tell me what they would really say. They almost always ask why I asked that particular question. My answer is always the same, "I just wanted to see how real you are and whether you would answer the question honestly."Even if a woman doesn't share the specific expletives that would come out of her mouth if she hit her thumb with a hammer, the question lets her know that you want her to be herself.

Men often approach a woman by formally introducing themselves. This is a mistake. When a man's first words are, "Hi, my name is Charles," a woman will feel obligated to tell him her name, which she may not be ready to do. By engaging her in light conversation for a few minutes or until the two of you have danced together, you give her an opportunity to be comfortable before placing her in a position of feeling that she has to respond to you. If she finds you interesting, she will introduce herself first. By doing this, she is confirming that she is friendly, comfortable, and possibly interested.

When a man talks to a woman, what he says is not as important as how he says it and how he reacts while he is saying it. According to experts, what we say accounts for only 7 percent of our communication. The tone of our voice accounts for 38 percent. Our body language accounts for 55 percent.

Frequently looking into a woman's eyes while you talk to her is an important part of expressing your interest. Another technique, however, is much more effective in creating a feeling of chemistry, subliminal rapport, and trust. This technique is called *mirroring,* which involves your responding to a woman's communication and body rhythms in an identical but subtle manner. An example of mirroring often occurs when a couple is sitting together and talking at the bar or a table. If the woman leans toward the man and looks into his eyes while the two of them are talking, for instance, there is a special feeling that occurs when he mirrors her body movements by also leaning toward her and looking into her eyes. The warm feelings may further be intensified if the man takes one of the woman's hands in his, followed by her taking his other hand in hers.

Mirroring a woman's communication and body rhythms does four things for you:

1. It confirms that you are attentive and interested in her, not in yourself.

2. It allows her to lower her guard and subconsciously feel more relaxed in your company.

3. It establishes rapport and trust. Women are more likely to trust a man who is like them.

4. It gives a woman the wonderful feeling of being in sync with you.

Rule of Thumb . . .

Mirroring works very well for a man when dancing with a woman. Women enjoy dancing with a man who mirrors their body movements.

While you are mirroring a woman's communication and body movements, be alert to what she is doing. If she responds to your communications and body movements, she is signaling that she enjoys following your lead.

Approaching a Woman Who Is in a Group

A group of women will sometimes go out to a club together. If you are interested in dancing with or talking to one of them, it is usually difficult to get one to leave her friends. Rather than ask one particular woman in the group to dance, approach the group confidently and with a smile and ask,

"Would one of you ladies like to dance?" Look at the woman you are interested in first, then pan the table and be sure to look at each of them as you ask the question. Now, don't be surprised if the biggest and least attractive woman in the group takes you up on your offer. Dance with her anyway! Later, it will be easier for you to approach the group again and ask the particular woman you are interested in to dance. Don't be a klutz on the dance floor, and don't be too flashy with your dance moves. If the group responds positively to your dancing, you have a good chance of getting a dance with the woman you are interested in. I have seen men use this technique and eventually end up sharing the table with the group of women and having a great time.

If a woman who is with a group of women sets her sights on a man, the others in the group will usually support her and help her attract the man's attention.

Rule of Thumb . . .

In a group, a woman who shows interest in a man may not be as interested in him as she is in getting attention in the presence of her girlfriends. Rarely will women in a group compete for a man's attention.

Understanding and Handling Rejection

Men who are capable of being quite aggressive and competitive in sports, the military, and business are often terrified to approach women in a club or bar. A man's fear of rejection is directly associated with the male ego. A man's need to achieve and be in control feeds his ego. In clubs and bars, women are in the position of power. When they reject our approaches, we are robbed of the fundamental part of our mental framework, and the fragile part of our ego is exposed. Since others in the club may witness the rejection, the experience is doubly humiliating. The fear of having our egos publicly battered can be so overwhelming that many men will avoid putting themselves in a position to be rejected. Others believe that if they hang around a woman long enough, she will eventually like them.

If you approach women in clubs and bars, you are going to be rejected. No man is successful 100 percent of the time. Rejection does not mean you aren't desirable. It usually means either that you are not a particular woman's type or that you may have approached her the wrong way. While rejection can be awkward, it does not have to be terrifying. Don't be afraid to fail!

Rule of Thumb . . .

The best way to overcome fear is to have the courage to confront it!

There are four distinct attitudes as to how men view and manage the possibility of rejection.

Some men seek opportunity, not safety. Several years ago, I knew a man whose success with women at our local club was envied by many of us who observed him. He was not particularly handsome, and he didn't even own a car. He traveled by motorcycle. He was always approaching different women, and from my observation, he was considered to be more successful than not. One night I asked him why he was able to succeed as often as he did. His answer was simple. He approached women with the strategy of an insurance salesman. While he was rejected most of the time, the occasional yes he received made it all worthwhile! He just was not uptight about the possibility of being rejected. In his words, "Every no I receive is just part of the process to get to a yes."

The more often some men are rejected, the better able they are to deal with it. The home run kings in baseball often have the distinction of having the most strikeouts. Although a batter may strike out, the possibility of hitting a home run is always possible, as long as he is swinging. I have watched men change a woman's mind by not allowing her initial rejection to send them to the dugout. Men with attitude have probably learned to handle rejection and have the ability to turn rejection into opportunity. Chances are good that they will connect with a woman almost every time they go to a club.

Some men will move only in the direction of their standards and preferences. My club friends know that I love to dance. Most of them also know that I generally only ask classy women to dance, women I could imagine dating and making love to. There is no question that sex is on all men's minds when they go to clubs and bars. Many are interested only in picking up a woman for the night. A smaller number may only be interested in dancing and having some innocent fun. An even smaller percentage may be interested in meeting date prospects.

The possibility of rejection is reduced when a man is accustomed to approaching the type of woman he prefers and has been successful with. He is more comfortable and consequently more confident. His approach is suited to the type of woman he prefers. He understands how she thinks, is patient, and will not automatically go into an ego-protection mode if a woman is not receptive to his initial approach.

The higher a man's standards, the smaller the field of prospects will be. If there are no suitable prospects in the club, this type of man is perfectly content to go home alone and try another time. Rarely will he settle for anything less than what he prefers.

Some men focus on small successes. The self-confidence required to meet women in clubs and bars requires a combination of courage, action, and risk. A man may be interested in a particular woman but isn't quite confident to approach her. In order to bolster his self-confidence to approach this woman, he may initiate conversation or dance with other women who are receptive. If he is unsuccessful with the woman he is really interested in, he can resort to his earlier successes. The risk for this type of man is that he may miss his window of opportunity. Other men may approach a woman that he is interested in during this time when he is building his self-confidence.

Some men seek safety. Most men in a club or bar have a low threshold for rejection, and therefore rarely approach women or initiate conversation with them. Once they have had a couple of drinks to build their confidence, they might approach a woman and ask her to dance. If they are turned down, they are ruined for the night. Most of these men then resort to holding the walls up, getting drunk, or leaving the club or bar.

Men who have this attitude about rejection seek a sure thing. They are capable of responding to a woman who approaches them. They can't afford to be picky, however. They have to be willing to settle for whatever comes their way. They usually leave the club with less esteem and less money than they came with.

Another form of rejection is called *X blocks the square, or pussy blocking*. This happens when a woman acts as a shield or barrier for a girlfriend that a man is attempting to pursue. The girlfriend may or may not be interested in him, but it doesn't matter. The woman doing the blocking has made a decision that she does not want you to pursue her girlfriend. She will block your efforts for one of three reasons:

1. She doesn't want to be ignored or feel left out.
2. She knows her girlfriend has had too much to drink and is not exercising good judgment.
3. She knows her girlfriend is not interested in the man.

When X blocks the square, a man's best bet is to simply let the woman he is interested in know that he would like to see her again and then be gracious enough to leave. If the woman is interested in him and has a means to contact him after the night is over, she usually will.

Rule of Thumb . . .

Never stay where you aren't welcome.

Rejection of an indirect kind occurs when a woman is interested in a man for reasons that differ from his. Men have a big head above their neck and a little head below their waist. There are times when the little head does our thinking for us, and we do stupid things. Some men, for instance, will spend an inordinate amount of time and money on a woman because they think they have a chance to leave the club with her. Women are smart. Some know they can drink free all night, if they play their cards right.

Some men make the mistake of pursuing a woman who is receiving attention from several men. Not only are the odds stacked against them, but other women will notice and conclude they are desperate.

A smart man realizes when a woman's interest differs from his. He knows that sometimes he has to pull in his net and cut his losses.

THE ATTRACTION

Men have to work hard to succeed at flirting, but women are born with the ability to flirt as a means to signal their interest in and attraction to a man. Imagine you are in a club or bar and a woman approaches you and asks for a light. Is she flirting or just looking for a light? My first suspicion would be that she is flirting. Why? The first tip is that she approached me. If we had been sitting at the bar together, I might think differently. The second tip is that most clubs and bars have matches openly available for their patrons. The third tip is the woman could have asked one of the bartenders for a light. Bartenders always have cigarette lighters just for this purpose.

Here's another scenario. You are standing alone and enjoying the music the deejay is playing when a woman comes up and asks if you would like to dance. Is she flirting, or does she just want to dance? If she is relatively inattentive while the two of you are dancing, she is likely only interested in dancing. If, on the other hand, she focuses on you and not on her dancing, she is probably flirting. You have to know what to look for to understand whether a woman is flirting and interested or whether she is not.

One of the best flirting tips to know about women is that savvy women know men love hearing the sound of their own names. If a woman you don't know has taken time to learn your name and uses it when she talks to you, she is obviously interested in you. If she makes an effort to touch one of your arms while she is saying your name, she is flirting at her masterful best!

A woman often signals her attraction silently. She may seem awed while talking with a man. She may stare at him, while she moves to the beat of the music. If she is a little shy or unsure of herself, she may make herself *conveniently* available by walking past him or by standing or sitting near him. The most important thing to know about a woman's signals is that they are often subtle. Here is a list of the most common signals a woman may send to indicate she is attracted to a man:

- She smiles and laughs a lot.
- She raises her eyebrows while looking at him.
- She turns her body toward him and crosses her legs.
- She focuses all her attention on him and appears to be oblivious to everyone else in the club.
- She rubs the stem or the rim of her cocktail or wine glass.
- She rubs her hair, chin, cheek, hands, or arms while looking at him, listening to him, or talking to him.

- She plays with her jewelry.
- She talks to him by leaning toward him and whispering into his ear.
- She mirrors his communication and body movements.
- She places one of her fingernails between her teeth.
- She gently bites her lips, shows her tongue, licks her lips, or touches her front teeth with her tongue.

Rule of Thumb . . .

If a woman is uncomfortable or nervous, she may touch her nose, neck, or the top buttons of her blouse repeatedly. These are signals that a man is coming on to her too fast or too aggressively.

Closing the Sale

Once a sales prospect has shown interest, professional salespeople ask themselves four questions as part of successfully closing a sale.

1. Do I know what type of close I am seeking? For instance, do I desire to get an order, have the customer agree to a second meeting, or have the customer agree to accept a sample shipment of our product?

2. Have I removed the customer's objections?
3. Have I recognized the window of opportunity and taken advantage of it?
4. Did I talk myself out of the sale?

After a woman has signaled her attraction, a man should ask himself similar questions, when he is attempting to close on an opportunity with her.

- What type of close are you seeking? Do you want her to go to your place after you leave the club? Do you want to go to her place? Do you want to kiss her in the parking lot? Do you want to have breakfast with her? Do you want to get her telephone number or e-mail address? Do you want her to accept your telephone number or e-mail address?

- Have you removed her objections? Does she feel safe and comfortable with you? Does she trust you? Does she see you as a man who has something to offer?

- Have you recognized the windows of opportunity and taken advantage of them?

- Are you talking yourself out of the sale?

Rule of Thumb . . .

Focus on making a variety of incremental closes.

By getting a woman to make a series of small decisions, you will have a better chance of making the big close. Small decisions might include persuading her to accept a request for a slow dance, allowing you to join her at a table, getting her telephone number, walking her to her car, kissing her before the night is over, or getting her to agree to meet for breakfast just before or after the club closes.

During an annual sales meeting one year, my company's CEO had this message for our national sales team: "You can do everything else right, but if you don't ask for each order, you will lose out to your competitor." I have watched men fail to seize an opportunity with a woman in a club because they didn't ask for the order when they had the opportunity.

One night, a friend of mine met a woman at a popular club in Boston, while he was visiting from Dallas. They hit it off well and enjoyed dancing and talking until thirty minutes before the club was ready to close. When he felt he had closed on the smaller opportunities during the night, he went for the big close at midnight by asking, "So, what can I cook us for breakfast in the morning?"

Rule of Thumb . . .

When you think you have an opportunity to close, be direct but respectful.

In an environment of dim and colorful lighting, loud music and alcohol, a woman's emotions can cause her not to think clearly. If you fail to close during a window of opportunity, you can be assured that other men have noticed the woman you have been talking to and may attempt an end run on you. This is especially true if the two of you remain in the club until after midnight.

If your goal is to get a woman's telephone number for future conversation, there are two ways you can do it. A man can ask for a woman's telephone number, or he can wait for her to offer it.

Women will give their telephone numbers only if they feel comfortable. It is easy to scare a woman away by asking for her telephone number before she is ready to give it to you. Men who are too aggressive, too pushy, overly generous with compliments, or too interested in sexual conversation send up big red flags. Women will usually not give these men their telephone number or they will give them a wrong number.

I rarely ask a woman for her telephone number. If I am interested, I will make sure she knows that I would very much like to talk to her again as a friend. If she too is interested, chances are good that she will give me her phone number and perhaps her e-mail address. The best thing about this technique is that the idea is hers, not mine.

An alternative to asking a woman for her telephone number is to give her yours. Doing so lets her know you want to hear from her and talk to her again. Some women would never ask for a man's telephone number, even if they were interested in him. By giving a woman your home telephone number, however, you will likely hear from her within a week, if she is interested. Remember to express your desire to talk to her again as a friend.

A woman may give a man an incorrect number to appease him. There are a couple of ways to tell if a woman is giving you an incorrect telephone number. When you ask for a telephone number, have her tell you the number verbally while you write it down. Intentionally read the number you have written incorrectly and then say something like, "I'm not sure I wrote it correctly. Would you tell me again?" Or read the number you have written back to her and transpose two digits. If she has given you a made-up number, she may not be able to recite the same number a second time. Consider this a clue she may have given you an incorrect number.

Some women have memorized a false telephone number to give out to men they aren't interested in. Since most of us rarely call our own telephone numbers, we usually have to stop and think about it for a moment. If a woman gives out a number too quickly, be suspicious. The number she gives you may be like playing the lottery—the chances of all seven digits being correct is unlikely! When Robert thinks he is receiving a bogus telephone number from a woman, he will excuse himself on the pretense he is going to the men's room. He then goes to a pay phone and calls the number to see who answers. If he gets no answer or he gets the voice mail of the woman who has given him the number, he will go back into the club and resume talking to her. If a stranger answers, however, he will return to the club and ask the woman if she lives alone, has a roommate or a babysitter. If he suspects the number she gave him is an incorrect number, his conversation with her is like the Gulf War. It's over!

Don't talk yourself out of the sale by losing track of your objective, which is to impress a woman you have met and make her comfortable with you. Don't be overly talkative, for instance, while you are dancing with a woman. Chances are she can't hear you anyway. Even if she can, your talking may interfere with her dancing. Communicate with your body and facial expressions. Don't discuss the bad experiences you have had with other women who may be present in the club. A woman will conclude that you will do the same with her. Don't bad-mouth other men in the club. If you can establish yourself as being a cut above them, you have already beaten out most of your competition. Making other men look bad diminishes your advantage and also makes you look bad.

Chapter 11

Touch Techniques

Touching gives a man an opportunity to establish physical contact and receive some immediate feedback if a woman finds him appealing. Rarely will a man react negatively if a woman he is interested in touches him. In fact, he hopes it would happen that way more often. For women, however, being touched constitutes an act of intimacy. It must be done in the right way, at the right time, and by the right man. While touching can produce positive reactions from a woman, it also can lead to problems.

Nonsexual Touch Techniques

Let's say you have met a woman at a club. You make small talk and ask her a couple of questions. Before long, the two of you are engaged in conversation. You now have four opportunities to touch her hands, arms, or shoulders in a nonsexual way.

Touch to establish rapport. After you have talked for a few minutes, formally introduce yourself by name, and then extend your hand to shake hers. It is a mistake to introduce yourself to a woman you do not know before you have her attention. After you have her attention and you introduce yourself, a handshake is a most effective way to establish additional rapport.

Touch to emphasize a point. Emphasize a point you are making while talking to her by lightly touching her forearm.

Touch to express agreement. While the two of you are talking, listen for opportunities to respond to something she says by saying to her, "I know what you mean," "I agree with you," or "I feel the same way." While you are agreeing with her, simultaneously touch her hand, arm, or shoulder.

Touch to show affection. If a woman has responded positively to your nonsexual behavior, the next step should be to touch her a little more intimately but still nonsexually. You may lightly rub her forearm, lightly squeeze her upper arm, or simply hold her hand while lightly rubbing the back of it with your other hand. If you are in a position to look at her, eye contact will add to the effect and heighten her response.

Sometimes, a woman gives silent permission to be touched in a nonsexual way. She may touch your hands, arms, or shoulder while talking. She may hold your hand as the two of you approach and leave the dance floor.

Nonsexual touching can be both innocent and suggestive at the same time. If done properly, it can engage a woman's mind, incite her imagination, and produce emotional responses. Your main objective should be to further communicate your interest and look for an emotional response, without getting a negative reaction. Women do not like men who are too touchy or intrusive. If you do get a negative reaction, you are getting too close!

Sexual Touch Techniques

Gently touching a woman's face, neck, waist, hips, thighs, and legs can be sexual without being lewd. These areas, however, should be considered off-limits, unless a mutual sexual attraction exists. Even then, however, sexual touching should be done discreetly. Your objective should be to sexually arouse the woman without being too obvious or putting her in an embarrassing situation.

The opportunities and techniques for sexual touching vary, depending on whether you are sitting, standing, fast-dancing, or slow-dancing, and depending, most importantly, on the woman. I strongly emphasize that you have to be your own judge when it comes to sexual touching. The techniques that follow will not work on every woman!

If the woman is sitting on a bar stool and you are standing in front of her or beside her, one technique is to stand close enough to allow one of your legs to touch one of hers while occasionally touching one of her thighs above the knee with a hand.

If she is sitting on a bar stool and you are standing behind her, gently rubbing the sides of her neck or the back of her neck below her hairline can be sexually arousing.

If the two of you are sitting at the bar together, a sexual touch technique is to gently rub the inside of the thigh closest to you just above the knee with the tips of one or two fingers.

If you are dancing to a fast song, turn your back to her about one-third of the way through the song and keep dancing for fifteen seconds. She may move her body closer to you and do a booty rub. If she doesn't move closer within fifteen seconds, she is likely not going to respond, so turn back around to face her. If she does move in closer to you, let her *work that booty* for ten to fifteen seconds before turning around and facing her. If she does not turn her back to you to give you the same opportunity, place your hands on her waist and slowly turn her around. If she allows you turn her around, keep your hands on her waist or hips and do your booty rub discreetly for no more than fifteen seconds.

If you are slow-dancing with a woman, begin by holding one of her hands. A third of the way through the song, place both hands around her waist. If she places her arms around your neck, she is comfortable dancing close. Rub the back of her neck below her hair. Whisper into her ear if you must talk while dancing.

If the two of you are standing and facing each other, take a drink. Stand close enough to her so that when you lower your drink, the back of your hand discreetly touches one of her breasts.

It's in His Kiss!

In 1964, Betty Everett recorded a Top 40 hit written by Rudy Clark entitled "The Shoop Shoop Song (It's In His Kiss)." The song was rerecorded by Cher in 1991 and used in the movie *Mermaids*. The lyrics are a testament to the significance of a man's kiss to most women.

A woman may be sexually aroused by her sense of hearing, but kissing is often the first act of intimacy that stirs her emotions and endears a man to her. In a woman's mind, a tender, romantic kiss conveys a message that a man really cares about her. Women believe men who are good kissers tend to be good in bed, and men who are lousy kissers tend to be lousy in bed. Men believe the same to be true of women.

Carla cautions men not to underestimate the effect that kissing has on a woman.

Rule of Thumb . . .

If you don't want a woman to become emotionally involved with you, ***don't kiss her!***

If you do decide to kiss her for the first time, and you think she will be receptive, kiss her softly and with feeling, and when she is not expecting it. If she is comfortable enough not to stop you, she will remember this surprise for a long time.

Chapter 12

Club Friends

Clubs and bars can be a playground or a battlefield for friends. There is usually a group of regulars in most clubs and bars on weekends. Women often develop real friendships that extend beyond the club. Males use the term "friend" more loosely, however. Their pseudofriendships are usually confined to the club; they rarely know much about each other outside the club. Men who spend time together in clubs and bars generally refer to each other as buddies or partners. They rarely know the other's last name or where he lives or works.

Women believe that men brag about their sexual conquests to their club buddies. It's true that most men do kiss and tell, but seldom do they do so with other men who go to the same club or bar. Usually they will do so only with friends or buddies who have no connection to the club or bar.

Rule of Thumb . . .

Where women and sex are concerned, men don't trust other men! They are careful not to give out too much information, especially to their club buddies.

Club girlfriends often seek each other's approval when they meet men they are attracted to. One of the girlfriends will introduce a man she is interested in to her club girlfriends. If the girlfriends like him, she will like him even more.

If a woman feels good about a relationship that has developed with a man she has met in the club or bar, she will tell her club girlfriends everything about the relationship, and in explicit detail! Her girlfriends will know how well a man kisses, how long and wide his penis is, and how good he is in bed!

Rule of Thumb . . .

Younger women tend to share more details of their sexual experiences than older women do.

Although one-night stands aren't as common as they were during the pre-AIDS era, they still occur. If a woman has a one-night stand, she will usually tell only her closet club girlfriend. If the experience was a good one, she will want to share it. If she feels bad following the experience, she may seek her girlfriend's support. Sometimes a woman will share the details of her sexual experiences with her club girlfriend to make her jealous!

Friendship Killers

The glue in men's friendships is loyalty and respect. There is an unwritten law among men that when it comes to pursuing women in clubs and bars, unless they have discussed it in advance, one man will not pursue a woman that one of his friends is interested in. If a man finds himself in a situation where his little head is doing his thinking, however, this law can be breached. When this happens the friendship will end. The pursuit of a woman that a male friend is also interested in is the ultimate display of disrespect. Not only will a man have a problem dealing with this, but he will also feel victimized. His ego will not allow him to accept defeat by one of his so-called buddies.

Often, these matters worsen because men make the mistake of telling a third party about their conquest or are indiscreet in their actions.

Rule of Thumb . . .

Disloyalty and disrespect are the primary reasons club friendships between men end.

Women bond more closely than men; the glue in their friendships is honesty and trust. The primary reason a woman ends her friendship with a girlfriend is when her girlfriend lies.

Where men are involved, there is an underlying competitiveness between most women, even if they are friends. If men in a club always pay more attention to one woman than they do her girlfriend, the friendship between the women will eventually be affected. The problem will not be because one or more men came between them. The real problem will be the envy that results when one of them is continually chosen over the other.

It is important to note the difference between envy and jealousy. Envy involves two people, but jealousy always involves a third person. When a woman envies a girlfriend, she secretly admires something about her girlfriend that she would like to have for herself.

Sometimes a woman will become envious simply because her girlfriend shares too much information about the intimate relationship she has with a man who frequents the club. A late-night Dallas radio personality used to describe himself as a panty-snatching, booty-slapping, big-toe-sucking, deep-tongue-kissing, earlobe-licking, hickey-leaving bad boy! If a woman goes into this much detail in describing a lover to other women who come to a club, other women might be tempted to experience this for themselves!

If a woman is insecure in her relationship with a man at the club, she may distrust her girlfriends and avoid sharing intimate details of her relationship.

While men kiss and tell, a woman may never know if one of her girlfriends has been intimate with a man that she is involved with. Women aren't caught as often in their indiscretions as men are.

Rule of Thumb . . .

Lying and envy are the primary reasons club friendships end between women.

Chapter 13

Club Couples

Couples who go to clubs together face unique challenges. A prominent, well-built sports figure occasionally came to a club that a group and I frequented a few years ago. He only approached women who were with a man. More often than not, the women he asked to dance recognized him and usually said yes. Sometimes, however, the women's dates or husbands became jealous. The opportunity to meet a famous athlete, however, was usually enough to offset any real problems. Besides, the athlete was 6 feet 5 inches tall and weighed 260 pounds!

One night, I asked the athlete why he concentrated his attention on women who were with a man. He told me that he was not interested in meeting a woman in a club for any reason other than to dance. Women who were in the club with a man were simply less risky! Surprisingly though, he also admitted that his competitive spirit was at play. He received a thrill and a boost to his ego by stealing the attention of a woman from the man she was with.

Certain men, not just professional athletes, will disregard the fact that a woman is with a man and particularly so if the woman is dressed provocatively, dances provocatively, appears to be disinterested in the man she is with, or simply appears to be approachable. For some men, these are signals that the woman is not really happy with the man she is with or that she is promiscuous.

Rule of Thumb . . .

If a man attempts to hit on a woman who is in the club with another man, he usually does so because he thinks he has more to offer her or will treat her better than the man she is with.

Diane and Paul were a couple and were regulars at a club. Of the two, Diane was more extroverted, even flirtatious. She usually wore leather or short skirts with high-heeled shoes and no pantyhose. When she and Paul were in the club together, it was obvious that he didn't like the attention she received from other men; however, he always appeared to be comfortable and confident in his relationship with her. One night, Diane was in the club with her sister, without Paul. A gentleman I will call Kenneth approached Diane and told her that he had noticed her in the club with her husband, who, he then said, "is one lucky man!" Diane corrected Kenneth by telling him that the man she was usually in the club with was not her husband but her boyfriend. She then confessed that she and Paul were having some problems, and she needed to get out for the night to think about things. Kenneth must have done everything right because he and Diane danced and talked for two hours before she decided it was time to go home. Kenneth asked if he could walk her to her car. She agreed, and as she got ready to get into her car where her sister was waiting, she and Kenneth exchanged a passionate kiss in the parking lot. Kenneth asked if he could see her again. She told him that as much as she wanted to, she couldn't until she knew what was going to happen with her and Paul.

The following weekend Diane and Paul had made up and were at the club together. Kenneth was also at the club. Paul knew that Kenneth liked Diane, but he did not know of the kiss in the parking lot. Kenneth watched Diane from a distance most of the night, but he did not say anything to her until she and Paul were about to leave. While Paul closed his bar tab, Diane, who was a little tipsy by now, walked to the ladies' room. On her way back to meet Paul, Kenneth intercepted her near the rear exit of the club to tell her how nice she looked, and that he really would like to see her again. As he spoke to her, he held one of her hands. Paul walked back toward the exit to meet Diane, where he noticed Kenneth holding her hand and talking to her. What should Paul do?

1. Tell Kenneth to get lost?
2. Ask Diane to explain what is going on?
3. Ask Kenneth to explain what is going on?
4. Try to befriend Kenneth?
5. Leave the club without Diane?
   (Remember she has had one too many drinks.)
6. Take her other hand and say to her, "It's time for us to leave"?
7. Wait for Kenneth and Diane to finish their conversation?

First of all, Paul should avoid confrontation. Telling Kenneth to get lost or asking him or Diane to explain what is going on might be the way we did things in high school. None of these, however, is appropriate behavior between adults in a public place, especially a club or bar, where men are going to be men.

Expecting a man to befriend another man who is hitting on his woman or waiting for another man to finish talking with his woman is like pushing a car uphill with a rope; it ain't gonna happen!

Assuming Paul is mature, he is really left with only two choices: either leave the club without Diane in her inebriated state or approach her and tell her it's time for them to leave.

Carla once told me, "Women have relatively few real choices in this world, but the men a woman gets involved with are strictly her choice!" Diane contributed to the problem by encouraging Kenneth the week before. Tipsy or not, it was her responsibility to put him in his place. She should have been a more responsible drinker.

Paul chose to leave the club alone for two reasons. First, he knew Kenneth had been hitting on Diane on other nights they were in the club together. He also felt that Kenneth had displayed the ultimate form of disrespect by hitting on Diane while he was present. The primary reason he chose to leave, however, was that he did not trust Diane, who he had come to believe was too much of a flirt. Paul felt that the incident justified his ending the relationship. He later told me that he would have handled things differently if he did not know Kenneth or if his feelings for Diane had been stronger.

Couples must accept mutual responsibility to avoid the temptations and complications than can exist in a club or bar environment. The man must control his wandering eyes. The woman must dress appropriately. Men in a club or bar tend to have the attitude that if a woman is willing to *show it,* she is willing to *share it!* A couple should act and look like a couple and avoid being too attentive to other men and women in the club, including friends or acquaintances.

Rule of Thumb . . .

Don't take sand to the beach!

If you are a regular at a particular club, it is usually not wise to take a date to that club. In addition to the possibility of receiving unwanted attention, there may be an old flame in the club, someone who is interested in you from past visits to the club, or someone you have expressed an interest in before. These possibilities only serve to arouse suspicion, create jealousy, or result in missed opportunities.

The most dangerous situation for a couple is when one of the two is a regular and the other is employed by or owns the club or bar. In these types of relationships, there is too much that can happen and be misconstrued by one or the other. An off-duty police officer who works at one of our local clubs met and became romantically involved with a woman who was a regular there. As a condition of their relationship, they agreed that she would discontinue frequenting the club that he worked at. When they wanted to go out dancing, they selected a club in which neither of them had any individual ties or associations.

Jealousy between men and women occurs when a third party invades the territory and causes self-doubt and a feeling of not being worthy. Jealousy is a man's way of saying, "I don't trust you, and I don't think I am good enough to keep you from being interested in other men." Jealousy is a woman's way of saying, "You act as if you could have more feelings for her than you do for me."

If a woman asks a man a question about an ex-girlfriend that she does not want an honest answer to, she will probably receive an answer she doesn't want to hear. For instance, asking a man if he still has feelings for an ex who is in the club is a question a woman should probably not ask. If he answers yes, the woman asking the question will feel threatened. If he answers no, she will think he is lying.

Rule of Thumb . . .

Don't ask a man a question about an ex-girlfriend in the club if you do not think you will like the answer.

Have you ever wondered why you are unsuccessful pursuing certain women in the club, but when you are there with a date, the same woman or women who were not interested in you before will act as if they are interested in you now? They may come over, speak to you, and ignore your date. Some may be bold enough to ask you to dance, even though they can clearly see you are with a date. Some may even slip you a napkin with their telephone number or a message on it as you walk by to go to the men's room.

When a man is in a club with a date, he does not present a challenge to other women, but his date does! Even if other women in the club aren't interested in him, his date may present a challenge for some women to prove they can compete with her. Do not fall for this trap. If you are in a club with a date, do not be disrespectful to her or make her feel uncomfortable by responding to the flirtatious and manipulative efforts of other women. If other women are that interested in you, there will be another opportunity to pursue them when you are alone!

When a woman knows she has lost a man she was emotionally involved with to another woman, she is going to have some issues if her ex-boyfriend shows up at the club with his new lady. The ex-girlfriend will feel that she has been played and may become vindictive and vengeful. Depending on how a woman learns that her boyfriend is involved with another woman, she may display a flair for the dramatic and make a scene in the club.

Rule of Thumb . . .

Women have to see their competition.

If woman thinks she can compete with an ex-boyfriend's new lady, she may show up at the club, usually with one or more girlfriends, while her ex-boyfriend is there with her. The ex-girlfriend will likely be dressed to kill. She will make sure the ex-boyfriend notices how good she looks, and she will flirt with other men to make him jealous. She may want to win her ex-boyfriend back, or she may want to lure him in so that she can dump him like he did her! After seeing her competition, a woman will not likely attempt to contact her ex-boyfriend for a while, if she does not think she can compete. If she thinks she can, she will compete!

Men, if you are going to take a lady to a club that is an ex-girlfriend's stomping ground, show her the respect she deserves and explain the situation early. Do not allow your date to be placed in an uncomfortable or compromising situation.

Here's a final note on the subject of club couples. If a woman feels she has been lied to, mislead, or dumped by a man who continues to come to the club, she may attempt to get even by telling his buddies some unflattering things about the him. Her criticism may be aimed, for instance, at the size of her ex's penis or his premature ejaculation problem.

Rule of Thumb . . .

Depending on how angry she is, a woman may exaggerate her criticism of an ex-boyfriend.

Chapter 14

Last Call and Closing Time

"Last call! Last call for alcohol!" When these words blast through the speakers in a club or bar, it's time for some to leave, time for some to jump in line to order that last beer or cocktail, and time for others to put forth their best effort to hook up with someone. Some men's and women's behavior can change radically after the last call has been given. Men who were too shy to approach women earlier in the night may become bold. Men who were not in the club or bar earlier magically appear after the last call has been given in search of women who have had too much to drink or women who appear desperate. Women who were relatively reserved may also become more aggressive, or, in some cases, a little more reckless with their sexuality.

Sometimes, the last drink or two before closing time brings out a part of our personality that is suppressed when we are sober. Brenda and Rick were friends and had known each other for more than ten years. They had never dated but were part of the same circle of club regulars. They had danced and talked off and on one Saturday night in their usual manner but nothing serious. Rarely did either of them stay at the club until closing time, but on this particular night, they stayed until the deejay announced, "Last call! Last call for alcohol!" They ordered one final drink and continued to talk. Brenda surprised Rick by asking, "Why don't we go out together sometime?" She then admitted that she had wanted to go out with him for a long time but was afraid to ask. "In fact," she said, "I would not have asked tonight if I had not had a little too much to drink." Brenda was not drunk, however; she had had just enough to drink to say what was on her mind. She and Rick did go out together several times and are still the best of friends.

There is a saying among men that "women become more attractive just before closing time." The truth is that by 1:30 or 2:00 in the morning, a woman's looks aren't the most important criteria for the men who are still around. By then, men have forgotten about their preferences and are in their *minimum standard mode*.

I asked several men this question: "If it is thirty minutes before closing time and you have the opportunity to leave the club with an attractive woman who is very large or an unattractive woman who has a nice body, which would you choose?" Almost all men responded by saying they would choose the unattractive woman with the nice body. While discussing this subject at a club one night, Charles commented, "You can drink a woman pretty, but you can't drink her skinny!" Another one of the guys commented, "It's going to be dark if I get her into bed, so her looks won't matter."

Some men actually prefer a woman of size. David, for instance, is not attracted to small women at all. He says, "The bones are for the dog; the meat is for the man!" Another friend of mine, who likes larger women, says, "Big women are built for comfort; small women are built for speed."

Rarely will a woman accept an invitation to go home with a man she has met in a club or bar these days. Women are more cautious; they have to be. It can happen, however, particularly if a man and a woman are already acquainted with each other.

When a man invites a woman from a club to his place, it is important that she feels welcome, comfortable, and relaxed. She will notice how he has decorated, the colors he has chosen and, most importantly, how clean his place is.

Men generally prefer dark rooms and dark colors, a throwback to the caves in prehistoric times. Dark colors may be conducive to romance in the bedroom. A man's living room, however, will be more conducive to romance if it is well decorated and well lighted.

The most important room to a woman in a man's house, condo, or apartment is his bathroom. A woman who is a first time guest will usually overlook that a man's living room, kitchen, and bedroom aren't well decorated. After all, a man is a man, and most aren't into decorating and dusting. These rooms should at least be clean and neat. Women, however, like their bathrooms bright, clean, and decorated with matching colors. Besides being just a bathroom, this room is a special place where a woman makes herself look and feel beautiful and sexy for a man. Here are some tips to keep in mind:

1. Make sure the toilet, the shower and the bathtub are spotless. Be thorough. Nothing will turn a woman off more in your bathroom than diarrhea shots left under the toilet seat!
2. Have potpourri and at least one fragrant candle displayed.
3. Have at least one large bath towel convenient. Women love large, fluffy, white bath towels.
4. Always have a new roll of toilet paper, a new bar of soap, bubble bath, a new toothbrush, toothpaste, and mouthwash available.
5. Have a couple of quality brands of hair shampoo and lotion on hand.

It is also a good idea to have female hygiene products available—but not openly displayed—in case a woman needs them while visiting you.

Neither should women's perfume be openly displayed. Women have their own preferences for fragrances. If a woman you are having over for the first time sees a female fragrance in your bathroom, she will think you entertain other women. Maybe you do, but you don't need to advertise it!

Last, but not least, do not keep condoms in the bathroom that your female guests will use!

Conclusion

The nightclub and bar scene is not for everyone, but neither is bungee jumping or eating sushi.

Clubs and bars are playing fields. As such, the interaction between men and women involves some gamesmanship. Like any game, there are obstacles, offensive and defensive players, time limits, and penalties. Knowledge, skill, conduct, attitude, appearance, a good game plan, and conditioning separate those who enjoy the experience from those who don't. A parting thought to keep in mind is that everyone in a club or bar is there for one or more reasons. If you understand the reasons particular men and women are there on a particular night, the object of "the game" is to overcome the obstacles, create interest, meet, interact, and have fun.

Final Rule of Thumb . . .

If the game is not in you, play it long enough and it will get in you!

Appendix I

Tips for Drinkers

Since clubs are responsible and liable for over serving alcohol to their patrons, they will stop serving a person who, in their opinion, has had enough to drink. Some clubs have gone a step further and will provide transportation for patrons who may be too drunk to drive.

While these efforts help keep drunk drivers off the roads and highways, state DUI and DWI laws have become less and less tolerant of drinking and driving. In many cases, two mixed drinks aren't enough for a bartender to stop serving a patron, but they may be enough to get you arrested.

If you are going to drink, here are some tips and a rule of thumb to consider:

- Take two aspirin before you to go to a club.
- While you are there, go easy on mixed drinks that contain alcohol, carbonated water and sugar (e.g., rum and Coke, 7 and 7, bourbon and Coke, gin and 7). The combination of carbonated water and sugar mixed with alcohol remains in your system longer than other drinks do.

- There is an old saying: *beer and whiskey, a little risky, whiskey and beer, have no fear*. If you are going to drink beer and liquor, drink the liquor followed by beer, not the other way around.
- Approximately thirty minutes before you leave the club, drink a glass of club soda, seltzer, or other non-sweetened carbonated liquid.
- Several clubs offer unlimited nonalcoholic beverages at no charge to the designated driver in a group. This offer is usually not advertised, so you may want to ask your bartender.

Rule of Thumb . . .

Law enforcement officers look closely for drunk drivers after the clubs and bars close. Your chances of being stopped are not as great if you leave the club by 1:00 A.M.

Appendix II

Topless Bars and Gentlemen's Clubs

There are six primary reasons some men spend time and money in topless bars and gentlemen's clubs, *where the men drool—and the women rule.*

1. There is usually a variety of classy-looking, provocatively dressed women. Men love to look at a variety of women!
2. A man can go at his convenience.
3. The women have to approach men!
4. They are safe; bouncers are quick to act, if needed.
5. There is no competition from other men. Dancers usually focus their time and attention on one man at a time.
6. Men don't feel that they have to say or do the right things to keep a woman's attention. This is especially true for shy men!

In most topless bars and gentlemen's clubs in the United States, a dancer can work if she is eighteen years old, but she cannot drink.

Rule of Thumb . . .

Underage dancers are usually required to wear a wristband so that the bartenders and waitresses will know she is underage.

There are first-, second-, and third-tier topless bars and gentlemen's clubs. Many of the first-tier clubs feature elegant atmospheres, suitable for business meetings, full lunch and dinner menus, and VIP memberships. Some even have beauty salons, gyms, and boutiques for the dancers on the premises.

Second-tier topless bars and clubs often conduct contests to recruit new dancers. The first-tier clubs don't have to recruit new dancers with contests, because most of the dancers in these venues are professionals. It is not uncommon for some of the dancers in the first-tier clubs to travel a circuit and dance in two or more clubs, sometimes in different cities, during the week. In some first- and second-tier clubs, well-known adult film stars will make scheduled featured appearances.

Most topless bars and gentlemen's clubs have three or more stages. There is a rotation process by which each dancer does stage dances on each of the stages. After a dancer has completed her stage rotation, she can visit with patrons for conversation and lap dances. Depending on the number of dancers working a particular shift, each usually has at least an hour between stage dances. When onstage, the dancers usually pick the songs for the deejay to play. They perform their first stage dance fully dressed and then strip for a second dance on the same stage. While a dancer is onstage, patrons will walk up to the stage one at a time, where the dancer will meet them and dance in front of them for about a minute, after which time they will tip her $1-$5. Once a dancer has completed two dances on the main stage, she will rotate to the other stages and dance topless.

Rule of Thumb . . .

If you think you might want to buy a lap dance from a particular dancer, her stage dances provide an opportunity for you to see her with her clothes off before you spend your money.

Dancers make their money by performing personal lap dances. The price of these personal dances range from $5 in some third-tier bars and clubs to $20 in the first-tier clubs. If a patron pays by credit card, there usually is a $5 surcharge per dance.

Now that I have described for the uninitiated how the dancers earn their money, let's get down to the business of the business. A dancer's job is to create a sexual fantasy for the patrons. They spend a great deal of time to look the way they look. To them, the job is just that, a job. It can be a very lucrative job, however.

Dancers appreciate men who accept these venues for what they are: a source of entertainment. Some of the men, however, find it difficult to separate fantasy from reality. Some are a little too aggressive. Some expect more from the dancers for the money they spend. There is a creed among dancers that greedy customers "will get screwed, but they won't get laid!" If so inclined, dancers are able to persuade greedy men to spend a lot of money only to leave drunk and with a bad case of the blue balls!

Men enjoy receiving personal attention from the dancers but don't want to feel like they are being hustled. Some dancers will work the bar or club by spending only a few minutes with a patron. If they fail to get him to spring for a lap dance within their allotted amount of time, they move on to the next prospect. The most successful dancers, however, will invest some time to make themselves good company first and then solicit dances.

Let me describe two types of male prospects. The first is an overweight, unattractive guy who is horny and willing to spend some serious cash. The second is a clean-cut, handsome, professional man who might not spend as much money but treats a dancer with respect. Which prospect will a dancer usually prefer? The answer depends on the dancer. If she is strapped for cash and only interested in making as much money as she can on a given day or night, she will likely choose the first prospect. A dancer who is financially secure, on the other hand, or one who prefers to build a clientele of regular clients will likely choose the second prospect. If he buys at least one lap dance, it will be a good one because the dancer will actually enjoy dancing for him. An experienced dancer knows that if her first dance is good, a man like the second prospect might want another. If he enjoys the quantity and the quality of time the dancer spends with him, he might become a regular customer and might even bring other friends or business associates into the club in the future.

Certain days and certain times are better than others to go to topless bars and gentlemen's clubs. Generally speaking, men will receive more time and attention from dancers who work during the day. They don't expect to make the kind of money the night dancers do, because most clubs aren't nearly as busy during the day.

If you like the nighttime action, Tuesday, Wednesday, and Thursday are the best nights of the week to meet a topless dancer. The men in the clubs on these nights are generally just regular guys out for a little entertainment. Dancers will spend more time with a regular client, and they won't try to hustle as hard to make a lot of money as they would when the club is more crowded. Most of the night-shift dancers begin work at 7:00 P.M. The best time to go to topless clubs to possibly meet one of them is after 10:30 P.M. By then, most of the married men have spent their secret stash of mad money and are on their way home. If the dancers have made some good money, they may be more willing to have some fun.

Rule of Thumb . . .

A man's chances of meeting and dating a dancer are better at second- and third-tier bars and clubs.

Like any club, Sundays and Mondays are usually dead nights. Dancers may be working these nights because they have to at the request of the management, not because they want to. If this is the case, they aren't going to put their best foot forward. They just want their shift to be over so that they can get some sleep. You will likely find the most beautiful dancers and more variety on Friday and Saturday nights. The weekend nights, however, are all about money! The dancers' objective on these nights is to make as much as they can, so they generally won't spend a lot of time with a patron who is not spending money, preferably a lot of it!

The most difficult dances for a topless dancer are her very first dance and the last dance she performs before leaving the business. The first dance is difficult because a new dancer is somewhat afraid and unsure about herself. Dancing topless can be a little embarrassing and humiliating for a neophyte. The last dance for a dancer who is quitting the business is difficult because she knows she will no longer have the opportunity to make easy money.

Rule of Thumb . . .

When you first meet a dancer, always ask her how long she has been dancing. If she's new at it, you probably won't get as good a dance from her as you would an experienced dancer.

All the personal business between dancers is taken care of backstage. Behind the scenes, some dancers will scheme to get some men to spend more money. Some fight and bicker over the order in which they will perform their stage dances. A small-breasted dancer, for instance, usually will not want to follow a large-breasted dancer onstage. Occasionally, a dancer has been known to put itching powder or some other irritant in another's T-back out of anger or jealousy. Dancers also are very protective of their sources of revenue. There is an unwritten rule between dancers that one will not approach another's customer to try to get lap dances. In most of the better clubs, there is a house mom behind the scenes who keeps an eye on the dancers, helps them with their outfits, their hair and makeup, and encourages them to do their best when they are onstage.

If a second dancer joins a man and another dancer who are seated together, the two dancers likely are friends, or they may be working as a tag team. Tag teaming may be done for one of two reasons. If a man is dropping some serious cash or running up a large credit card tab, one dancer may be willing to share the windfall with one of her dancer friends. Two dancers may also tag team to take care of a rude, obnoxious, or bothersome man who is not spending money but whose behavior is not bad enough for him to be bounced. If you are curious about the specific tag team techniques that dancers use to take care of bothersome men who are not spending money—perhaps you are one of them!

About the Author

Rodney Battles is a native of Fort Worth, Texas. He now resides in Hurst, a suburb between Fort Worth and Dallas.

A 1980 graduate with a BBA from the University of Texas at Arlington, he has been employed by a telecommunications equipment manufacturer for thirty years. Considered by his peers and management to be a classic overachiever, Rodney has held over fifteen positions in engineering, operations, marketing, and sales during his career. He began his sales career in 1983 and has been twice inducted into his company's President's Club since its inception in 1993.

An astute observer of people, who also enjoys dressing well, dancing, and dating, Rodney has enjoyed the urban club scene for portions of four decades, dating back to the late '70s.

He also enjoys computers, traveling, photography, reading, writing, listening to old school R&B and jazz, and fine dining.

Visit Rodney's Web site at http://www.rodneybattles.com.